Romanticism

A Reconsideration

Romanticism
A Reconsideration

edited by

N. M. ASTON

Reader and Head
Department of English
Nowrosjee Wadia College
Pune

PRESTIGE
in association with
Nowrosjee Wadia College, Pune

Published by
PRESTIGE BOOKS
3/28, East Patel Nagar
New Delhi 110 008

1999

ISBN: 81-7551-068-4

Composed by Pivot Computers, Delhi 110 006
Printed by Dhawan Industries Offset, New Delhi 110 028

Contents

Introduction

N.M. ASTON

I

As a part of the bicentenary celebrations of the publication of the *Lyrical Ballads* by William Wordsworth and S.T. Coleridge in 1798, we present this volume to our esteemed readers. The papers included in this volume consider the relevance two hundred years later of Romantic poetic concepts and their practice. Further, they assess how far modern advanced developed critical methods can bring out the relevance.

The Romantic movement which started around 1770 affected all the arts and culture in general, but in essence it was a reaction against the eighteenth century and concentrated in the imagination and the individual. The *Lyrical Ballads* marks the beginning of the romantic movement in poetry. Produced jointly by Wordsworth and Coleridge, the volume opens with Coleridge's "Rime of the Ancient Mariner" and closes with Wordsworth's "Tintern Abbey." The two poems can be said to contain in germ all the poetry of the nineteenth century.

In his "Preface" to the second edition of the *Lyrical Ballads*, published in 1800, Wordsworth explains that the principal object of these poems was to choose incidents and situations from common life and to relate them in a language actually used by men, and at the same time to throw over them a certain colouring of imagination whereby ordinary things should look extraordinary.

Wordsworth believed that the materials of poetry are to be found in every subject which can interest the human mind. In other words, there is nothing unpoetic or undignified about the material of poetry. He preferred to write about humble and rustic life because this life is more congenial to express itself more naturally and freely than in the sophisticated atmosphere of the town.

The *Lyrical Ballads* are written as experiments, to ascertain how far the language of conversation of real people is suitable for the purpose of poetic pleasure. In his language, Wordsworth revolted against the "gaudy and inane phraseology" of the eighteenth century poets. He insisted on using the colloquial language of the rustics because there neither is, nor can be, any essential difference between the language of prose and metrical composition.

But the most important point to note in this romantic manifesto is the emphasis on imagination. Though working in two different directions, natural and supernatural, the two poets (Wordsworth and Coleridge) were to achieve the desired result through one and the same instrument—imagination. And this imagination was to be in a larger sense the creative power. The poet, according to Wordsworth, is not a mere embellisher of truths discovered by other people, but a discoverer of his own truths. He is a seer, a prophet, who sees visions and communicates them to the world.

II

In his scholarly article "Romanticism Reconsidered," R.S. Kimbahune considers Romanticism as having a salutary influence on Indian literatures. He draws particular reference to the utterances and opinions of Hulme, Pound, Eliot, Leavis, Babbitt, F.L. Lucas and Barzun who were only too eager to magnify the shortcomings of Romanticism to condemn it as false, detrimental and something one can do without. Romanticism, as per Isaiah Berlin, is an imaginative creation of the truth of the object by the seeker, the poet or his self. Romanticism tries to attain the 'absolute.' He thinks that Wordsworth's "Preface" represents a declaration of literary independence.

In his article entitled "Romanticism and Classicism: A Note," L.S. Deshpande projects the view that despite the blatant condemnation of Romanticism by Hulme, Pound and Eliot, romanticism and classicism can be seen as two different irreconcilable attitudes or mental states inhering in the very nature of man. He adduces lines from Eliot's *The Waste Land* to show how romantic elements infiltrate into the very fabric of his 'classical' verse. His conviction is that for both classicism and romanticism, the highest ideals are the same—Truth, Beauty and Goodness.

A.M. Deshpande begins his article entitled "Romanticism and History" by asking a question, "what is romanticism?" Whether it is a conceptual category or a time-bound historical category or an epistemological category. Essentially romanticism was a rebellion against the Enlightenment theory of knowledge. Intuition and imagination were the two important romantic tools of historical investigation. Evolution of ideas was, according to the romanticists, a proper field of historical investigation. In fact, to the romanticists, history itself was an idea.

In his article "Romanticism and the Theory of History," C.R. Das elaborates how Romanticism emerged as a rejection of the eighteenth century enlightenment, rationalist value system. It refused to see the society as a stagnant entity and conceived it as an organic whole, historically evolved. In its attempt to romanticize, the primitive 'folk' past, it inspired thinking in every branch of knowledge. The result was the emergence of evolutionary sciences.

In his masterly article entitled "We and Romanticism," M.K. Naik points out how F.R. 'Leavis and Eliot condemned Romantic poetry in obedience to need of the time, that is, just as Wordsworth revolted against the 'inane' phraseology of the classical poetry, Eliot revolted against the affete romanticism of Georgian poets. Eliot himself was a poet in the Romantic tradition as evidenced in his poems *The Hollow Men* and *The Four Quartets*. Naik regards how in India of today, Indian poets like Nissim Ezekiel and Keki Daruwalla discredit the highly romantic and mystic poetry of Aurobindo. Arguing that it is impossible to offer an all-comprehensive definition of Romanticism, he attempts broadly to denote Romanticism as "a kind of art which enshrines a world-view shaped by a highly emotional, imaginative and transcendental approach to reality." He surveys Indian English romantic poetry and focuses on its rich indigenous heritage, thereby pulverising the Indian condemnation of Romanticism impelled by British prejudices.

By passing traditional eulogies showered on Romanticism, Vivek Phadke in his article "Is This What Romanticism Has

Done?" spells out how Romanticism failed to fulfil its mission. The early inspirers of Romanticism, William Goodwin and Pierre Joseph-Proudson and after them Mikhail Bakunin, had all favoured anarchism, preaching it in every visible form. Phadke opines that Romanticism has been far reaching in its indoctrinaire propaganda of violence, anarchy and secession, so much so that today Romanticism is anathema to many.

In his article on "Keats's Theory of Poetry and Eliot's Theory of Impersonality," K.S. Iyer opines that Keats's theory of poetry as it emerges from his letters and as illustrated in his "Ode to a Nightingale" is a fore-runner of Eliot's theory of impersonality as Keats also considered a poem to be a composition in a state of a complete disinterestedness of mind. The article builds up the argument to this effect, by relating Keats's three-dimensional aspect of poetry—his theory of poetry, his concept of beauty and his theory of negative capability—to a set of six premises drawn from Eliot's theory of Impersonality, to show that Keats's theory is by far, a classical view of poetry in the romantic age.

Robert Pinto's article "The Romantic Metaphysicals" is an in-depth study to relate the metaphysicals to the romantics. Both were revolters against conventions and used peculiar imagery, conceits, epigrams, paradoxes, hyperbole. Both laid emphasis on imagination and loved nature with same gusto. Pinto copies lines from the metaphysicals and the romantics to drive home his point that the romantics were metaphysicals in several respects.

Prabha Sampath's article "'On *that* side Idolatry': A Re-Appraisal of Romantic Criticism with Special Reference to Shakespeare" examines the contribution of Romantic criticism of a constructive nature. Sampath argues that the sensitivity and best appreciation of Shakespeare by the romantics helped to rediscover him to the contemporary age. Coleridge established the organic unity of Shakespeare's plays and Lamb, Hazlitt and others also made significant contributions. She concludes by saying that romantic criticism on Shakespeare influences twentieth century criticism and that the romantics have 'helped us to a profound understanding of the bard.'

Anjali Nerlekar's article "Unknown Modes of Being: Wordsworth's Poetry" is an attempt at refutation of the stand of pseudo-intellectual critics who consider Wordsworth as irrelevant today. Nerlekar traverses the length and breadth of *The Prelude* to substantiate her view that Wordsworth really matters today. She intersperses her argument with references from Wordsworth's poetry and the Upanishads in establishing the permeability and penetrability of beings into one another despite their separate existence.

A.T. Kenghe in his article "Wordsworth Reconsidered as Romantic Critic and Poet" evaluates Wordsworth as a democratic poet and critic. A fresh light is thrown on the classical restraint inherent in Wordsworth's process of poetic creation. Kenghe takes objection to Wordsworth's patent theory of poetic diction which sees no difference between the languages of poetry and prose by adducing lines from his poem "Tintern Abbey" to prove the contrary true.

Some of the articles in the present volume offer new insights and fresh interpretations. A new interpretation of Keats's "Ode to a Nightingale" by S. Kannamal arouses our curiosity. In reading this poem, the critic claims, the text speaks not of the Nightingale but of the intermediaries of experiences and contexts. This approach has a special significance for the records here because the scholar examines Keats's poem in the Indian socio-historical literary-cultural context.

Zeenat B. Merchant's article entitled "Shelley as a Visionary and a Rebel with a Cause: A Retrospect" attempts to reassess Shelley as a visionary par excellence and a radical thinker who wrote in an age which was unfavourably inclined towards him and his thought. Merchant argues, with copious references from Shelley's poems, that the poet was far ahead of his age in championing the cause of free will of the human being as a source of his perfectibility, striving for rejuvenation of mankind by affording scope to the intuitive excellence of our true nature for goodness rather than belief in Original Sin, taking up the cause of woman's emancipation, as a prelude to man being free, and the like. She considers Arnold's criticism of Shelley as an 'ineffectual angel' to be a misnomer for Shelley exhorts his countrymen in *Prometheus Unbound* to rebel against authority to usher in a new era.

A special feature of the present volume is that it seeks re-appraisal of the English Romantic period in the context of drama too. Muktinath Chatterjee in his essay entitled "Drama in the Romantic

Age" makes an extensive study of the dramatic principles enunciated by the Romantic writers and examines how far these were put into practice in their works. It focusses on Charles Lamb, more popular as an essayist, who etched his name as a critic of Shakespearean tragedy and Restoration comedy.

Contribution of the Romantic period to English drama is highlighted in yet another article, on John Keats's *Otho the Great* by Jibesh Bhattacharyya. According to this critic, Keats's first attempt at writing for the stage is the product of mature genius. Had he lived longer and continued writing for the stage, he might have matured into a successful dramatic artist.

III

It is obligatory on my part to express my sincere thanks and gratitude to Dr. R.K. Dhawan of Delhi University who inspired and encouraged me at all stages of the publication of the book. I am extremely grateful to the management of Nowrosjee Wadia College in general and Principal S.B. Tardalkar, Dr. S.R. Dastane, Controller of Examinations, University of Pune, Vice Principals Dr. A.S. Kalgaonkar and Professor M.M. Andar in particular for providing all possible help and assistance towards the publication of this book. My sincere thanks to Professor K.S. Iyer, Former Head, Department of English, T.C. College, Baramati, for his advice and encouragement in the preparation of this book. Finally, I express my appreciation and gratitude to Prestige Books for bringing out this book so elegantly and expeditiously.

Romanticism Reconsidered

R.S. KIMBAHUNE

I

Romanticism represents a major component in English Studies in India. As a student of comparative literature, I need not exaggerate the relevance of romanticism in the Indian context. More importantly, it is an absolutely unavoidable part of influence studies to gauge the literary traditions in the regional Indian languages. Very often our study of English literature is limited to texts in isolation with an historical orientation of a sort. But the text as a product of a certain ethos, as product of a certain socio-political and historic cultural complexities is very rarely pursued.

II

(a) "When the Sun rises, do you not see a round disc of fire somewhat like a Guinea?"
"O, no, no. I see an Innumerable company of the Heavenly Host crying: 'Holy, Holy, Holy is the Lord—God Almighty.'"

(b) I question not my Corporeal or Vegetative Eye any more than I would Question a Window concerning a Sight. I look *through* it and not *with* it."

William Blake

(c) I am not made like anyone I have seen; I dare believe that I am not made like any one in existence. If I am not better, at least I am different.

Rousseau, *Confessions*

(d) To be free is nothing; to become free is very Heaven.

Fichte

The English Institute brought out a collection of selected papers nearly 35 years ago, titled *Romanticism Reconsidered.* Northrop Frye had edited the book.[1] A thorough scholarly reconsideration was necessitated, perhaps, because of the diatribe against romanticism by the triumvirate of modern literature: T.E. Hulme, Ezra Pound and T.S. Eliot. Their contentions were as much a part of creative practice prompted by Pound's slogan "Make It New" as an attempt to win receptive space for their poetic experiments. Hulme's sentence, "I object even to the best of Romantics," was, in spite of his rigorous philosophical training, rather unfortunate. So was Eliot's urbane, tongue-in-cheek reference to Wordsworth in his celebrated programmatic essay "Tradition and the Individual Talent." But the temper did certainly generate controversy which proved salutary to a reconsideration of romanticism. Around the same time, in 1919 to be precise, Irving Babbitt's *Rousseau and Romanticism* was published. I do not know of any other book so mordantly anti-Rousseauist in its thrust and which holds Rousseau responsible for events that were to take place years after his death. Let me quote Babbitt: "Rousseau comes historically before the Revolution. He died eleven years before its outbreak and therefore can have felt none of the anxieties that assailed the men who came fifty years later, after the Napoleonic wars. Except for his sentimental yearnings, Rousseau's work is wholly destructive."[2] Estimations of Rousseau subsequent to Babbitt have, of course, thought otherwise. I dwelt on these details only to remind ourselves that T.S. Eliot was Babbitt's student.

As serious students of literature, we must be very clear as to whether we use the terms like romantic, classical or modern etc. as value terms or descriptive terms. Much of the confusion in criticism arises out of an absence of clarity. If we go all the way with Paul Valery, then there are no problems. Valery said, "It is impossible to think seriously with words such as Classicism, Romanticism, Humanism or Realism. One cannot get drunk or quench one's thirst with labels on a bottle." A good reminder, though obviously these terms are not merely labels. They pose real problems in literary history. Any understanding, any history of the human mind would be unthinkable without the configuration of concepts these terms represent. Here is Heinrich Wolfflin from his excellent

Principles of Art History:

> It is greatly to the interest of the historian of style first and foremost to recognise what mode of imaginative process he has before him in each individual case. . . . It goes without saying that the mode of imaginative beholding is no outward thing, but is also of decisive importance for the content of the imagination, and so for the history of these concepts also belongs to the history of the mind.

Note that apt, precise and magic phrase "the mode of imaginative beholding." Terms like vision, ethos, milieu, time-spirit that we frequently use attempt to approximate this accuracy of description.

Though we grant the historical-critical sanity of this approach, the problems of definition and conceptual discrimination remain unsolved. In 1948, for instance, F.L. Lucas reported to have counted 11396 definitions of the term romanticism.[3] It is difficult to share the computing gusto of Lucas, yet we cannot ignore the variety of uses to which the term has been put over the years. Jacques Barzun lists some of these in the 10th chapter of his book *Classic, Romantic and Modern*.[4] He sums up these meanings under four heads. The term romanticism has also retained its etymological inheritance and has been associated with 'improbability,' 'exaggeration' and 'unreality' or with adjectives like 'false,' 'fictitious' and 'imaginary.' Probably the word 'romantic' was first used to describe a certain quality in landscape painting—a certain hazy, dreamy quality captivating to the imagination. The emphasis, especially when the word 'romantique' was used, was on the emotional response evoked by a scene. But the focus changes when one begins to think about 'romantic' as an attitude, as a mode of perception, as a certain way of making sense of the world, that is a fundamental turn of mind favourable to imaginative and emotional richness of the self. Thus it was only natural that Friedrich Schlegel in 1797 characterised romanticism with three attributes: originality, creation and genius.

Another difficulty has to do with what Northrop Frye calls "the historical centre of gravity" romanticism has, approximately the period between 1790 to 1830, though some would like to extend it to 1850, the year of Wordsworth's death. This falsifies the treatment of romanticism as a set of timeless qualities. Because if we limit ourselves to that period, it is possible to quote Sappho, or the most poetic rejection of the poet by Plato, or Milton's Satan, or certain elements in the heroic dramas of Dryden to show similar qualities. To extricate ourselves from the danger of falling between two stools, Jacques Barzun proposed the concepts of "extrinsic" and "intrinsic" romanticism. Intrinsic refers to "human traits which may be exhibited at any time or place," whereas extrinsic is "the name given to a period in history because of the notable figures that gave it its peculiar character." Barzun's position is history-oriented and therefore very close to that of Rene Wellek who talks about Movement or historical period in terms of tendencies becoming predominant. Dominance of a set of norms, for Wellek, distinguishes periods in literary history. This, in fact, remains his major argument vis-a-vis the scholarly despair expressed by Arthur O. Lovejoy in his seminal essay "On the Discrimination of Romanticism." Lovejoy convincingly makes out a case for plurality in terms of national boundaries, difference of individual sensibilities, variety of styles and concerns. In view of plenitude of meanings, the word romanticism has, according to him, ceased to function as a verbal sign. Rene Wellek in his essay "The Concept of Romanticism in Literary History" attempted to refute Lovejoy's thesis. In a later day survey of scholarship that he calls "Romanticism Re-examined," Wellek attacked Lovejoy's extreme nominalism on the grounds of recent studies by continental scholars. With the coming of age of comparative literary studies, scholars began to see beyond similarities and also realised that the romantic period, for instance, in France, Germany and England did not coincide. Yet it was possible to see common denominators with desired degree of abstractions and generalizations. In the case of romanticism, according to Wellek, analogous concepts of the imagination, nature, symbol and myth provide the common denominators. It is against such a background that the phrase of Van Tieghem, the doyen of comparative literature becomes relevant and useful. He described romanticism as "a crisis in European conscience." The revaluation has equally strongly been characterised by Isaiah Berlin as "a shift in consciousness that cracked the backbone of European thought."

The implications are not difficult to trace. The backbone that Berlin talks about is "the possibility of a rational comprehension of the universe."

> Whatever the difference between the leading Romantic thinkers the early Schiller and the later Fichte, Schelling and Jacobi, Tieck and the Schlegels when they were young, Chateaubriand and Byron, Coleridge and Carlyle, Kierkegaard, Stirner, Nietzsche, Baudelaire there runs through their writings a common notion, held with varying degrees of consciousness and depth, that truth is not an objective structure, independent of those who seek it, the hidden treasure waiting to be found but is itself in all its guises created by the seeker.

I believe the passage brilliantly epitomizes the essence of romanticism, the seeker or the self or the subject, if you will and the imagination creating the sought, the truth or the object. Reality itself then is a construct of the imagination. In terms of polar oppositions, this yields two positions: one in which the subject and the object are two separate entities. The subject incessantly tries to reach out and merge with the object. And the second in which the object i.e. the world of external reality (the not-self or the other in modern-day formulations) is completely obliterated, a kind of extreme solipsism the next-door neighbour to insanity. Let us not mistake Wordsworth's "egotistical sublime" with narcissism for his notions are rooted in semi-mystical sources which many of his achieved poetic passages transparently articulate. But such moments are rare in romantic poetry. Incidentally the sprawling bardic energy of Walt Whitman or the eccentric, sinewy brevity of Emily Dickinson strongly celebrates this vision. Otherwise, romantic poetry mostly shows the self torn by a bridgeless dualism. The yearning for the absolute, what the Germans call *sehnsucht*, and the impossibility of attaining it, the desire to merge and be at one and the inability to do so, defines the source of romantic agony, the German Weltsmerz, the death-wish and the malaise that proved fatal to many a practising romantic artist. The absolute may take myriad forms: nature in the case of Wordsworth, the One in Shelley, the stasis attained by beauty and truth in Keats, the composite democratic self in Whitman, the oversoul in Emerson or simply God in its religious versions. If we compare these agonised articulations to Eastern Sufi and medieval Saint traditions, we see a remarkable difference. For the seeker, total union Sayyujya remains a distinct possibility. Therefore suffering and the constraints of the quotidian are shortlived in view of attainable unity sans temporality.

III

This aspect makes me suggest that the romantic discontent with temporality projects itself in the form of social revolt. Much of the severe criticism that a Shelley had to face was in a large measure, disguised attack on his dissatisfaction with the existing social order. Therefore, against the background of neoclassical framework, Wordsworth's description of the poet as Man speaking to men must have appeared strange. More significantly his objective proposed in *Lyrical Ballads* "was to choose incidents and situations from common life, and to relate or describe them, throughout, as far as was possible in a selection of language really used by men." I think the misplaced popularity of "the spontaneous overflow" passage in the "Preface" has made us blind to two things Wordsworth has done in the passage quoted above. He is making common run of humanity the subject of poetry—hence in his poems Michael, Peter Bell, Lucy, highland lass and such other characters—and perhaps what seems more revolutionary is the distinction he tries to institute between poetry that is literature-derived and poetry that is life-derived. He seems to anticipate the modern-day theories of poetic language. I believe he firmly says that the source of poetic language is the speech of the people, which decidedly happens to be the language of lived experience. Let me mention in passing that even Coleridge was none too happy with Wordsworth's formulations. In the same paragraph, Wordsworth justifies the choice of his subject. I am really surprised by the fact that I have not come across any objections to the contentions in the following passage:

> Humble and rustic life was generally chosen, because, in that condition, the essential passions of the heart find a better soil

> in which they can attain their maturity, are less under restraint, and speak a plainer and more emphatic language, because in that condition of life our elementary feelings co-exist in a state of greater simplicity, and, consequently, may be more accurately contemplated, and more forcibly communicated; because the manners of rural life germinate from those elementary feelings, and, from the necessary character of rural occupations, are more easily comprehended, and are more durable, and lastly, because in that condition the passions of men are incorporated with beautiful and permanent forms of nature.

But for a deeply and skilfully concealed attack on industrialisation and urbanization, the passage makes a series of assertions that Wordsworth does not bother to explain rationally. These seem to be articles of faith with him. And unless we attempt to support them on the basis of his poetic vision, we would find them hardly acceptable. The semi-mystical vision of Wordsworth perceived nature as an ideal order of piety and he elevated nature to the status of a Goddess to be worshipped. So the sublimity that Wordsworth talked about originated from "a greater knowledge of human nature, and a more comprehensive soul." From this point of view Wordsworth's "Preface" represents a declaration of literary independence.

I have so far avoided to mention how frequently romanticism is sandwiched between classicism and realism. Such contradistinctions are certainly useful, but in a limited way. It is possible to argue with Edwin Burgum that "liberty is opposed to the classical submission of the individual to authority, equality a denial of aristocratic hierarchy of social classes and abstract values and fraternity, a rejection of feudal disdain for democracy and common man." But this only highlights the political dimension of romanticism in its Rousseauistic formulation. From this perspective Shelley's characterization of the poets as "unacknowledged legislators of mankind" would be a political transformation of T.S. Eliot's notion of the poet's role in "purifying the dialect of the tribe."

Let me conclude with a brief reference to Fichte's statement

I used as an epigraph at the beginning. It implies an ethic of activity and seems to glorify failure. To become free defines a continual striving with no guarantee of success. Sacrifice sanctifies the cause. This position has a darker side that was visible in the Reign of terror, in the rise of Napoleon, in the cult of narrow nationalism and racial superiority, violent irrationalism, Nazism and Fascism. Isaiah Berlin has described this as "the negative heritage of romanticism" which outlines the traumatic shocks suffered by the Twentieth Century. The romantics articulated a world of enriched self and freedom, a world they wanted to live in and perhaps wanted all of us to share. Some of their insights and ideas found hysterical and distorted interpretations later. It would be historically unfair to hold them responsible because they had dreams for the whole of mankind.

NOTES

1. Northrop Frye, *Romanticism Reconsidered* (Selected Papers from the English Institute, Papers read in Sept. 1962), (New York, London: Columbia University Press, 1963).
2. Irving Babbitt, *Rousseau and Romanticism* (Boston: Houghton Mifflin, 1919).
3. F.L. Lucas, *The Decline and Fall of the Romantic Ideal* (Cambridge: Cambridge University Press, 1936).
4. Jacques Barzun, *Classic, Romantic and Modern* (New York: Achor Books, Doubleday, 1961 2nd revised edition of *Romanticism and the Modern Ego*, 1943).

Romanticism and Classicism: A Note

L.S. DESHPANDE

Just as a honey-bee-comb is the work of the honeybees, or a nest the work of the turtles, poetry is the work of the poets. Or what humming is to the bees or bellowing is to the cows, poetry is to the poets. So natural, so instinctive, and so impulse-driven. It is the voice of the Muse speaking through him, at once, in subjective and objective, abstract and concrete, particular and general, personal and impersonal, individual and universal terms. A child learns, using his legs first to stand, then to walk, and then to run, and, finally, to dance. What dancing is to the child, poetry is to the poet's mind. A sense of wonder pervades each's universe. The Freudian psychology looks upon the mind of man, as though it were, a poetry-making organ. Poetry is his "inner voice."

Very often, the art of poetry is seen as a thing divided against itself: the romantic and the classical. The twin aspects are shown as compartmentalized, as though in water-tight compartments, and as diametrically opposed to each other. The author of the present paper intends to propose that romanticism and classicism are, though antithetical, not mutually exclusive, i.e. where the one is, the other can't be. They are in his view, unlike in T.E. Hulme's, complementary, and not competitive. The two are not coalescent, it is true, but can be co-existent. One can see them, particularly romanticism, in different lights, since they happen to be multi-dimensional, rather complex, concepts with varying manifestations.

Such anti-romantic critics as T.E. Hulme, Ezra Pound and T.S. Eliot hail the twentieth century as the age of classicism. All of them are vehemently opposed to the romantic art. Ezra Pound clears the way for classicism through his highly individualized, and yet objective, imagistic conception of poetry suiting the needs of the contemporary society. Both T.E. Hulme and T.S. Eliot are critical of romanticism, the one mildly but quite reasonably, but the other bitterly, and quite unreasonably, with or without provocation. What Wordsworth calls "a spontaneous overflow of powerful emotions," Eliot ridicules, calling it "a dumping ground for emotions." Likewise, the "inner voice" of which Middleton Murry speaks so highly is disparaged as mere "Whiggery" by T.S. Eliot. Eliot, here, as nowhere else, is Torified in his hostility to romanticism which is more or less synonymous with liberalism.

Basically, romanticism and classicism are attitudes or mental states inhering in the very nature of man. The two can be studied as irreconcilable, rather as reactive phases, trends or movements in the dialectical process of the literary and cultural history of the nation. The one is in revolt against the other, overtly or covertly, in terms of their distinct as well as discrete elements and aspects, modes and techniques. Romanticism upholds the claims of intuition and asserts faith in absolute freedom. Classicism, on the contrary, upholds the claims of reason insisting on an order (as opposed to chaos) and due obedience to authority. The one believes in the infinite, while the other in the finite. However, a poem can be studied either as predominantly classical with an awareness of romantic elements interspersed in or about it or as pre-eminently romantic with an awareness of classical elements dispersed in or about it. To illustrate the case, see how Milton's Satan, a classical character, figures out as a romantic spirit in the first two books of *Paradise Lost*. Satan humanized is Satan liberalized, freed from the clutches of God and Heaven. Thrown into the hell, its "fiery lake," Satan recovers from "the thought both of lost happiness and lasting pain" and in a persuasive speech addressed to Beelzebub, he says:

> The mind is its own place, and in itself
> Can *make a Heaven of Hell, a Hell of Heaven. . . .*
> To reign is worth ambition, though in Hell:
> *Better to reign in Hell, than serve in Heaven.*

And yet again, sarcastically addressing his followers, the rebel angels:

> Awake, arise, or be *for ever fallen.*

See, likewise, how Eliot, a staunch advocate of what is called impersonal poetry, conceals his personal experience of youthful years as a keen yachtsman in the lines 418-22 of *The Waste Land* sings in a lyrical voice:

> . . . *The boat responded*
> *Gaily*, to the hand expert with sail and oar
> The sea was calm, *your heart would have responded*
> *Gaily, when invited, beating obedient*
> *To controlling hands.*

The italicised parts indicate how the romantic elements infiltrate into the very fabric of the classical verses.

One notices, on the contrary, how Keats attains "negative capability" and sounds almost classical, particularly in such odes as "Ode to Autumn" and "Ode on a Grecian Urn." Mark the classical note in the lines quoted below from the concluding part of the latter:

> "*Beauty is Truth* and *Truth Beauty*" that is all
> Ye know on earth, and all ye need to know.

Earlier in the poem comes Keats's aphoristic line:

> *A thing of beauty* is a *joy for ever.*

What we as readers perceive in these lines is a kind of sensuous impersonality realized through the poetic device of objectivising the subjective emotional experience. Eliot, through his use of persona, as in "Gerontion," seems to share it with Keats.

Neither romanticism nor classicism is an awful disease or a revolutionary philosophy. The former looks at the inner, the ideal, and the infinite, while the latter at the outer, the real, and the finite. When the idea manifests itself, through highly imaginative flights, idealistic terms, it looks romantic. See bow Wordsworth works in this direction and achieves the desired effects:

> . . . with an eye made quiet by the power
> Of harmony, and the deep power of joy
> We *see into the life of things.*

Right on his way, he finds

> . . . . tongues in trees, books in running brooks,
> Sermons in stones, and *good in everything.*

See how Eliot moves in the opposite direction to work out his effects: The idea, when treated classically, wraps itself in the realistic garb. The Thames's daughter dazed at the bitter experience of being raped, sings of her failure and frustration to meet the situation:

> On Margate sands.
> I can *connect*
> *Nothing with nothing*
> The broken fingernails of dirty hands.

Thus it may be observed that the highest ideals of the romantic art are none other than those of the classical art—Truth and Beauty, and Goodness, if you like to add to, for there cannot be poetry, even for the romantics, without Good Sense. A romanticist is one who looks upon man as "essentially good and an infinite reservoir of possibilities" while a classicist sees him as what he is—"limited" and "finite." "Progress" is the keyword of the romantic ideology, while "stability" is that of the classical.

The classicist, as opposed to the romanticist, is, in T.E. Hulme's words, "an extraordinarily fixed and limited animal" whose nature is absolutely constant. It is only by "tradition" and "organization" supported by "scientific thinking," that "anything decent can be got out of him."

The romantic poetry is inimical to the mundaneness of the mundane reality, the worldliness of the world. Read, for example, Wordsworth's sonnet, "The World is Too Much with Us." It is unconcerned with "here" and "now." It looks forward towards the future.

The Universal Spirit it embodies imbibes humanistic values. In short, it is an active, dynamic principle.

Romanticism is an avowedly progressive ideology in the sense that it is at odds with everything orthodox or conventional. It aims at man's self-inspired, dignified survival through an all-enveloping chaotic darkness. A romanticist knows no God or Heaven, but sees god in Man and heaven on the Earth. He is "the worshipper of Nature" and, as such, has his faith in one religion, that is, Universalism, which is far different than what He holds it to be "a spilt religion." The romanticist "jumps" into that abyss, while the classicist abhors such a risk. That is why, in the light of the extravagance that so often characterizes the romantic verses, T.E. Hulme is justified in pointing out that, in the classical verses, "even in the most imaginative flights, there is always a holding back, a reservation."

An image haunts the poet, whether classical or romantic, and takes possession of his mind. Originally, it is a line from Ariel's song in Shakespeare's *The Tempest* and Eliot uses it twice in the same poem for different purposes. But the fact is that not only Eliot but his readers also are so enamoured of it. The line containing the image goes thus: "Those are pearls that were his eyes." It creates a visual picture which "presents an intellectual and emotional complex in an instant of time," Pound says, and further adds: "It is better to present one image in a lifetime than to produce voluminous works."

A poem is a poem, whether romantic or classical, because of the emotional experience it presents. Rich and complex as this experience is, it gives the poem its life—its sound, colour and form. The emotion in poetry is, in Eliot's words, "significant," in Coleridge's "vital." The truth is the same, but the approaches are different, far less different than are usually supposed to be. The truth in art means sincerity of emotion, without which no great work of art can exist. What after all matters in poetry is emotion. Pound once said: "Only emotion endures."

The romantic poetry is deep-rooted in "the vague sensuousness" as opposed to what T.E. Hulme calls "the dry hardness" of the classical verses. Who can forget Byron's small poem "She Walks in Beauty" or Shelley's "Music When Softer Voices Die"?

The point is made clear, when you put it side by side with Pound's "In the Station of a Metro." Both the types present interesting word-pictures, but interesting for not only different but also opposite reasons. The one is vague or blurred, while the other clear, precise and accurate. The vagueness of the former tends towards the infinite, while clarity of the latter towards the finite. It is so because the romantic art is born out of the Unconscious and the classical out of the Conscious.

T.E. Hulme calls the romantic literature "a literature of wonder" but it is a misnomer to call it so. He sees wonder as a temporary state. Yes, it is true, just in one sense, while, and perhaps more important, it is a normal, ever-renascent, permanent emotion—just as pity and terror in Aristotle. The sense of wonder is due to the poetic vision, a sudden revelation of the hidden and the mysterious in life and the world around. It is, in short, enlightenment. All literature is the literature of light—the romantic, of the celestial light, and the classical, of the terrestrial light. The one spiritualizes the secular (Note: "The sounding cataract" is a haunting passion in Wordsworth) and the other secularizes the spiritual (Note: "Ganga" is "sunken" in T.S. Eliot) going beyond the worn-out, established creed or religion.

Bibliography

M.H. Abrams, *A Glossary of Literary Terms* (A New Prism Indian Edition with a Supplement; Bombay: Orient Longman, 1994).

David Lodge, ed. *20th Century Literary Criticism: A Reader* (London & New York: Longman, 1972).

Rene Wellek and Austin Warren, *Theory of Literature* (Harmondsworth: Penguin, 1962).

Romanticism and History

A.M. DESHPANDE

What is Romanticism to a historian? Is it an ideological category or is it a historical category bound in space and time? There is no denying the fact that historical thinking has been deeply, and I believe irrevocably, influenced by the romanticist ideas. It is true that the histriographers identify a specific school of historians as the romantic school, implying thereby that the list of historians supplied under this heading and the period during which such histories were written, exhausts the conceptual category known as the Romanticist history. Such a view is tenable if we accept that romanticism is a purely historical category bound in space and time. But it becomes suspect the moment we look at it as just an ideological or a purely epistemological category in the historical context.

Romanticism as an epistemology was not an accident. As Russell puts it, it was "a revolt against received ethical and aesthetic standards."[1] History writing during the period between the Renaissance and the mid-eighteenth century laboured under the infuence and impact of the Enlightenment conception of knowledge. The discoveries of the universal laws of Nature in the physical world overawed the philosophers and historians as it did the other creative thinkers. It became almost an aphorism to believe that all universe is governed and regulated by immutable laws of nature and human nature and behaviour is no exception to it. Since no such laws could be discerned in history, it came to be considered as irrational and arbitrary. "Caprice of history" became the laughing-stock of the Enlightenment world to the extent that Descartes did not consider history as being a proper subject of knowledge.

The net result of such a view was disastrous for history. Continuity, the most important component of historical thought, was totally ignored since history came to be perceived as a series of episodes unconnected with each other. Each episode was a compartment and each compartment an end in itself, an independent entity as it were, unconnected with either its past or future. Time ceased to be a dynamic force and history was condemned to be a 'dead past.'

The serious impediment that made history redundant and meaningless was the Enlightenment conception of human nature. Like all matter in the physical world, human nature was also considered to be uniform and unchanging. Laws applying in one instance were expected to be applicable in all other similar instances. If one apple fell from height x in time y, then all apples at height x were rationally expected to fall in time y. If it did not happen, then it was irrational since it was arbitrary. Since all knowledge was a systematised body of information from the perusal of which it was possible to make a confident prediction of the future, any arbitrary and irrational instance could not be a proper subject of knowledge. On the other hand, if it was not arbitrary then observing one apple fall was good enough to establish a general and universal law of gravitation. Observing hundred apples fall was one experience repeated hundred times, therefore redundant and meaningless. In the context of the then-prevalent theory of knowledge, history found itself caught on the horns of a dilemma from which it could not get off almost throughout the Enlightenment.

Romanticism challenged this mechanized approach. Its greatest contribution to the theory of knowledge was to think of knowledge, as an experience internalised rather than a mere external observation. It thus laid the foundations of a theory of cognition based not only on observation but mainly on perception. Human knowledge therefore is a series of such perceptions. The main concern of the romanticists was to understand the nature of all individual experiences as distinct from generalised experiences.

An observation becomes an experience through the medium of perception. But for perception to be an item of knowledge what is required is intuition, an undefined mental faculty which is very individual. Intuition and imagination, therefore, are the prerequisites of any process of knowledge.

Imagination was essentially a product of collective memory of past experiences of an individual or a group of individuals. As such all imagination was essentially an historical experience. Knowledge therefore was possible only historically.

What was history to the romanticists? Most importantly history was not only the legitimate field of knowledge, but it was the only true area from where human experience could be understood. To appreciate the present, it was necessary to understand the past. History remained central to the general romanticist thought, in fact an aesthetic experiencing of the past became a major artistic device of the Romantic movement. (One only has to browse through Byron or Browning.)

The greatest contribution of the Romanticism to historical thinking was to look upon history as an organic whole and to treat various events in history as so many links in a continuous chain of events. An event ceased to be a self-contained, self-regulating entity in itself and acquired a causal character in the general—and also Universal—scheme of history. Like the early medieval clerics, the romanticists also believed that history has a purpose. But unlike the clerics, the purpose of history for the romanticists was not the unfolding of some divine scheme inscrutable to the human beings, but a scrutable march towards fulfilment and realisation of the self. History to the romanticists was a continuous whole with which the present was intimately connected. As such, history was a living organism and not dead wood for the curious to look upon.

History, as conceived by the romanticists, was very much a part of the present, a part of our being. It was essentially a process of Becoming. To understand history was to understand this process of Becoming. Since the process of becoming is not verifiable physically, we have to understand it as a progression of an Idea. This, of course, could be done only through educated imagination. Imagination was however, not an external tool of investigation but an internal device of understanding. Imagination would yield no significant results unless it became a tool of empathy. Sympathy with the subject-matter and empathy with the historical process of Becoming were the two most important epistemological tools that the romanticists used in their understanding of the past.

History was a source of knowledge. The romanticists looked

upon history as a store-house of natural experiences of human beings. Looking upon the human beings as a genre of the natural world of the universe, they became less interested in the actions of individuals and more in those of the groups and communities. Masses tend to be inert and generally move slowly. Like the changes in Nature, their changes are gradual and imperceptible, not sudden and catastrophic change in history, therefore, is evolutionary in character and not sudden. Nor is it arbitrary. It has a purpose, an objective for the change. All historical process is essentially teleological insofar as it prepares the present for a better future. The dictum that all history is the story of progress that dominated the nineteenth century historical thought, was a direct derivative of this romantic teleology. This concept of history as a record of progress, subsumes an objective for the progress. To the romanticists the objective of progress, the final goal of history, was the creation and evolution of conditions conducive to the best realisation of an individual. Liberty, equality and nationalism were the generally accepted conditions for such a self-realisation. To philosophers like Hegel or the Utilitarians, an orderly and benevolent strong State seemed to provide the required conditions. To Bishop Stubbs, it was to be the Rule of Law. Underlying all the different conceptions, however, was the strong faith in the evolutionary nature of history. Hence their preoccupation with the various genres of history viz. the constitutional, the legal, the literary etc. History thus became the growth of an idea or ideas, nay, history itself became an Idea. With such an approach to the past combined with the investigative tools provided by the physical sciences, romanticism leads us to what Collingwood calls "the threshold of scientific history."[2]

That Romanticism contributed immensely to our understanding of the nature of history cannot be gainsaid. It was a giant step in liberating history from the position of the handmaid to theology. It also was a successful movement to give history its legitimate place in the general body of human knowledge. But most importantly, it worked as a force that brought people closer to themselves through their past. It gave people a sense of sharing a common past that cut across class barriers. It helped create a strong sense of nationalism and national unity.

These achievements, great as they were, were also fraught with serious consequences to the world. As an European phenomenon it certainly was a notable achievement. But the national unity it fostered among the European nations, coupled with the market economy generated by Industrial Capitalism, was soon to degenerate into pure jingoism and naked imperialism. Byron's nationalism is nothing short of xenobphobia. The myth of the 'noble savage' so assiduously cultivated throughout this period was soon to change its character. The emphasis shifted from nobility to savagery. Kipling's plea to send forth the best that England bred to civilise the natives of the East who were 'half children half savages' was typical of the racialism that was logically to flow from the romanticist syndrome. It is a significant commentary on romanticism to underline the fact that it was precisely in those nations that romanticism flourished that racial hatred also became the state policy.

This happened because of two important factors. The appeal of the romantics was more to emotion than to reason. Instead of a reasoned argument, the romanticists preferred an emotional outburst. Russell tells us that "they admire strong passions, of no matter what kind and whatever may be their social consequences." The savagery of the Terror during the French Revolution was a romantic act.

On the other hand, romanticism as a movement created a value system of its own. Its emphasis on individualism and emotionalism led to an excessive self-indulgence. So great was this self-indulgence that even Kant and Hegel did not find it audacious to claim an end of history with the coming of the romanticist ideology. The self-indulgence of the romanticists was not only narcissism of the worst kind; it was also very violent and destructive. This predilection for violence of all and any kind led them to search for strong passions in history and all history became history of violence, what Barbara Tuchman would call the "March of Folly." Paradoxically, love was also a basic value with the romanticists. But then this love was not the 'karuna' of the Buddha nor was it the love of Christ. It was essentially an extension of the narcissism, a projection of oneself. It were the romanticists who made nationalism a melodramatic value. The entire 'resorgimento' movement was a melodramatic nationalistic movement in Italy. Its German counterpart was the 'kulturkampf' and the 'volkkultur.' Benito Mussolini and Adolf Hitler were logical and legitimate successors to romantic historians like Herder and Hegel.

NOTES

1. *History of Western Philosophy*, p. 675.
2. R.G. Collingwood, *The Idea of History* (London: O.U.P., 1946).

Romanticism and the Theory of History

C.R. DAS

Romanticism as a phenomenon betrays any precise definition. It can most popularly be looked upon as a historical phenomenon that represented certain disenchantment with the present bourgeois rationalism and a longing for 'the folk' i.e., normally the pre-industrial peasant and craftsmen who exemplified the uncorrupted virtue. However, this representation of romanticism as a phenomenon in the latter part of the eighteenth century and the early part of the nineteenth century cannot claim to explain romanticism in all its manifestations. Although romanticism refers to a phenomenon in France, England and Germany mostly during this period which manifested stringent reaction against mechanical rational bourgeois society, yet it could hardly provide any reasoned critique of the society. Further, romanticism cannot be viewed as a narrow reactionary movement, but a way of looking at things, a value that directly or indirectly influenced thinking for a long time in European as well as world historical tradition.

In art and literature, romanticism glorified the 'primitive virtue' and 'uncorrupted man' and sought to return to this primitive simplicity and virture ('the folk') as reflected in Wordsworth's *Lyrical Ballads*. It was hunted by the lost unity of man and the nature. 'The folk' was, in fact a romanticist creation and a revolutionary concept especially among oppressed peoples about to discover or reassert their national identity, particularly those who lacked a native middle class. But for those who were struck more by the folks's simple virtue of contentment, ignorance and piety the deep wisdom of its trust in pope, king and tsar, the cult of the primitive at home lent itself to conservative interpretation. It exemplified the unity of innocence, myth and age old tradition, which the bourgeois society was everyday destroying.

In the sphere of the sciences, the romantic mind was actively at work. The last decades of the eighteenth century saw two revolutions. The first was the brilliant pioneering work of the seventeenth and eighteenth century rationalists which established the equivalent of physical laws for human population. Its earliest triumph was the construction of a systematic theory of political economy. The second, stimulated by romanticism, was the discovery of historical evolution. The theory of evolution of the earth in geology, Darwin's theory of evolution of species (Zoonomia, 1794), Laplace's evolutionary theory of the solar system (1796), Lamark's systematic modern theory of evolution based upon the inheritance of the acquired characteristics (1809), Chavan's ethnology as the history of progress of peoples towards civilization (1787) were certainly inspired by romantic persuasion.

Social sciences too came under the influence of the romantic movement. They seemed to show a historised trend during this period. History was no longer rendered unnecessary and was not a simple chronological narration of events or dealing with the 'spectacles' of the past but an instrument necessary to understand the past. History was now viewed as an organic whole. The present was seen to have evolved out of the pace. It is, therefore, a process. The urge to understand the present through the past was overwhelming. This view of history liberated from the enlightenment attack, constituted the epistemic foundation for a long time from now. The effect was an epidemic of history writing in Europe in the first half of the nineteenth century. The most lasting result of this awakening was in the field of documentation. The most representative figure of this period was Leopold Von Ranke (1795-1886). His doctrine of scrupulous evaluation of primary records influenced historical activities. The contribution of the linguists and folklorists was in no way insignificant. Alongside this, the emergence of a new science, philology, the laws of which were fundamentally historical and which regarded evolution as its very core gave fillip to the romantic zeal.

On the whole, the romantic approach opened up a plethora of

activities in different spheres of society the most immediate recipient of which was history. Its rebellion against the enlightenment did lead to certain creative propositions insofar as it stimulated new enquiries in social sciences and led to a new hermeneutic tradition in Europe. But the most distinct and enduring impact of romanticism is visible in the area of historical reconstruction which was not only benefited now by its emerging heuristics but was gathering momentum as an important epistemic foundation. It is the German tradition of Natural philosophy that the idea of history received the best treatment. In Germany the classical liberalism was very weak and rival scientific ideology to the classical was most popular. The leaders in this tradition attempted to theorise history by fusing different strands of the time namely, enlightenment and romanticism, just as they fused rationalism with empiricism. The leaders who represented this tradition were Herder, Kant, Schiller and Fichte. The four philosophers of history established a new status of history by putting history in a hermeneutic tradition and treating it as the only source of knowledge. Their major concern was the idea of history. To all of them

a) history is possible and intelligible
b) the whole human history is organically linked
c) history is a progress to an end, the end being the attainment of universal rationality
d) history is not a mere narration of events but an explanation of necessary logical growth of mankind
e) study of history, therefore, involves greater intellectual activity—a philosophical reflection.

All four of them begin by looking at the relation between man and nature. Herder proposes an organic conception of nature and finds higher and lower organisms in it. He argues that human life is a process of elaboration of the long and inter-linked process of organic development of natural process. Man is a perfection of animal life and therefore, its nature is the perfection of animal nature. Herder puts man in close relation with nature. Logically this argument envisages a theological view of nature. Although he argues that with man, natural process comes to an end, still the process continues with man being an end in himself. Human history, which is nothing but a part of the natural process, by extension of his argument, is a process towards realization of man's rationality. Kant raises man to a dignified position, by subordinating nature to man. Human history is not subject to the laws of nature. When Kant talks of 'the plan of nature,' he uses merely a metaphor. To him 'plan of nature' is an idea without which human history cannot be understood. Here Kant constructs nature as an epistemic category. Even though Kant draws a parallel between the process of nature and the process of history, he makes a fundamental difference between the two by postulating mind at the core of the historical process. In his teleological explanation, Kant sees human history progressing according to a plan. The progress is unconditioned to conditioned. Human history progresses to an end, the realization of the universal rationality. Here Kant is referring to the possibility of universal history. To him what causes the progress is the human irrationality. In other words, the human past is full of folly, wickedness, selfishness etc. and since man is a rational being—something that man develops through his consciousness of nature and it laws—history is a process of its emerging rationale. Like Herder, he sees the end of history in future.

Schiller and Fichte share Kant's view that history is a progress. Schiller sees history progressing from savage beginning to modern civilization and like Kant advocates the study of universal history. But Schiller disagrees with Kant on the end of history. To him the ultimate aim of the historian is to bring out as to how the present has evolved out of the past. Historical studies cannot be extrapolated beyond the present. Schiller made a significant contribution by broadening the scope of historical studies to include art, religion, economy etc., from merely the study of political evolution. Fichte shares the views with certain modifications. Agreeing with Kant, he posits that history as a whole is unfolding of a plan and the fundamental ideas or concepts of various successive ages form a logical sequence. This is what helps him periodise history in a logical structure of thesis, antithesis and synthesis. The fundamental concept of history is rational freedom and freedom like any other concept must develop through stages. The stages he talks of are primitive stage containing freedom in the form of blind instinct, the stage of civil freedom and the last stage is that of revolution, seizure of government by the governed. For Fichte history ends in the present.

The most significant contribution of these theoreticians of history was in the field of philosophy of history. This tradition was founded by Kant during this period. Kant situates a mind at the core of historical process. He called it the 'thing in itself' (Noumenon). Events in history are created by human mind (intention) and therefore history cannot be merely a narration of such events and historical studies cannot be subjected to the laws of nature. Kant discussed mind not in its phenomenal aspects but as a 'thing in itself.' To him mind is intelligible as opposed to sensible. Therefore he requires his historian to put historical events to philosophical reflections. Significantly here, he talks of intuition as very important category of human mind (a priori). Kant identifies the essence of mind as freedom, not a mere liberty of choice but as autonomy, the power to make laws for oneself. Kant affirms that human beings are endowed by nature with capacities, the chief among which is reason. Reason is a guide towards the realization of rationality. Kant requires a Newton and implicitly compares himself with Hepler.

Schiller carries Kant's idea of philosophical reflection of history. Historical events are not merely the objects of cognition but require historical imagination and like romantics talks of sympathy needed to enter the constitution of an event in order to understand it. This is, in fact, an important improvement on Kant's idea. Fichte follows Kant in this direction and argues that the only way to understand as to how the present has evolved is by analyzing the present from where a historian can make an entry into the past. The categories of the historian are his and not of the past that he studies.

The eighteenth century contribution to the emergence of the theory of history is significant. In the new developments, the elements of romanticism are quite visible. The romanticist rebellion against enlightenment spawned a plethora of activities chief among them was the emergence of historical science.

Thus, the construction of romanticism as only a rebellion does no justice to the movement. Its constructive elements which resulted into phenomenal developments in evolutionary sciences and themisation of history, could hardly be belittled. The impact of this early development influenced Hegelian thought, Collingwood's 'Idea of History' and more importantly Marxist Social Theory.

References

J. Bronowski, *The Western Intellectual Tradition* (Great Britain, 1960).

C.H. Carr, *What is History* (London: OUP, 1964).

R.G. Collingwood, *The Idea of History* (London: Oxford University Press, 1946).

W.A. Galsten, *Kant and the Problem of History* (Chicago: University of Chicago Press, 1946).

G.P. Geech, *History and Historians of the Nineteenth Century.*

W.A Hobsbawn. *The Age of Revolution 1789-1849* (Calcutta, 1992).

J.T. Merz, *A History of European Thought in the Nineteenth Century* (New York: Dover, 1965).

We and Romanticism

M.K. NAIK

In this bi-centenary year of the publication of *Lyrical Ballads*, it would perhaps be appropriate to ponder our reception in India of Romanticism over the last half century and more. In England, as is well-known, Romanticism had already become a doubly dirty, twice-four letter word, when T.S. Eliot and F.R. Leavis began a systematic campaign in early twentieth century to devalue Romanticism and the Romantic poets, with Shelley as their favourite whipping boy.

T.S. Eliot, who personally found Shelley's personality, beliefs and poetry unpalatable, went on disparaging all three repeatedly. As W.W. Robson points out, "He [Eliot] makes it plain that he is reporting his personal reaction to Shelley; he lays no claim to judicial impartiality. But . . . these remarks . . . gave them, for many of his followers the force of a papal edict. Eliot's remarks were very influential. (They were to be reinforced a few years later by Leavis's chapter on Shelley in *Revaluation*). As a result, Shelley has become the least known of the major English poets. Younger school and university teachers took their cue from Eliot and Leavis, and their pupils did not properly get to know a poet who might have become one of their greatest friends. . . . To this day Shelley has not recovered the fame he enjoyed in the nineteenth century. A writer in *Essays in Criticism* (October 1975) notes that in Britain at least he is still out of favour."[1]

As for F.R. Leavis, he asserted that "Shelley's poetry is repetitive, vaporous, monotonously self-regarding and often emotionally cheap, and so, in no very long run, boring."[2] (In an earlier chapter, he concedes that Shelley "is a poet of undoubted genius," (111) but then, the logic of *Scrutiny* will not perhaps stand the scrutiny of impartial logic). Such a sweeping verdict might make one agree with E.M.W. Tillyard, who finds Leavis "a better critic when he encourages us to read Carew or Pope than when he puts Spenser or Shelley on the index."[3]

This condemnation of Romantic poetry had its own rationale at that time. Leavis wished to champion modernism in poetry and Eliot's revolt was really against the effete, faded romanticism of Georgian verse. Just as in the eighteenth century an artificial poetic diction had come to vitiate and deaden the language of poetry, now a romantic poetic diction with its conventional imagery appeared to have British poetry in a stranglehold. In his revolt against eighteenth century poetic diction, Wordsworth declared his intention to use instead "Language really used by men." This was precisely the quest of Eliot also during the early decades of the twentieth century. In fact, this is not the only point of correspondence between the Romantic poet and T.S. Eliot. It is now being increasingly recognized that Eliot himself is ultimately very much a poet in the great Romantic tradition. The intense emotion in "The Hollow Men," the confessional mode in his mature work and the agonizing quest for the transcendental in *The Four Quartets* establish his kinship with the major Romantic poets.

But of course, it is only with hindsight that we now realize the true significance of what was really happening during the nineteen twenties and thirties in England. The Indians of the day enjoyed no such advantage. Besides, the colonial syndrome had crippled their critical faculties. The masters at Cambridge and London had spoken; their word was final. One recalls how a young Indian scholar, just returned from England, with the milk of his Oxford (or was it Cambridge?) degree bubbling fresh upon his lips, immediately insisted on removing both Milton and Shelley from the syllabus, because the 'masters' had pronounced an unfavourable verdict against both. (The reaction of this scholar, when Eliot later recanted in respect of Milton is not known).

This young Indian scholar was not alone in summarily dismissing Romantic poetry as unworthy of serious study. With the emergence of modern verse on the Indian poetry scene after Independence, it became highly fashionable to condemn the entire tradition of Indian English romantic poetry as virtually worthless. We were informed that "Indian verse in English did not seriously begin to exist until after the withdrawal of the British from India."[4] The editors of *Modern Indo-Anglian Poetry* (1959), a pioneering anthology of the new poets, condemned "the greasy, weak-spined and purple-adjectived 'spiritual' poetry and the blurred and rubbery sentiments of . . . Sri Aurobindo and declared that "the phase of Indo-Anglian romanticism ended with Sarojini Naidu."[5] Perhaps taking their cue from this, some of our 'modern' poets have since then steadily maintained a barrage of gun-fire against Indian English romantic poetry of the pre-Independence period. As in the case of Eliot, their assessment of this poetry is more in the nature of a critical strategy designed to justify their own poetic practice by implication than a balanced evaluation of a literary phenomenon to which they utterly fail to respond in the right spirit.

Consider some of the following pronouncements: Nissim Ezekiel tells us that in his opinion, "any one who thinks highly of Sri Aurobindo as a poet has no feeling for the English language."[6] K.N. Daruwalla candidly informs us that he has "read only one poem each by Toru Dutt and Sri Aurobindo," and "has no intention of reading any more."[7] He is, however, brave enough to assess conclusively the achievement of both these poets on the shaky basis of his confessedly slender acquaintance with their work, and proceeds to condemn Toru Dutt's "infantile manner" and dismisses Sri Aurobindo as "no other Indian poet was half as bad, none so nebulous or verbose."[8] (One would certainly like to watch Daruwalla's reaction, if a critic were to declare that he has read only a solitary poem by this poet, on the strength of which he would offer a conclusive assessment of his entire work.) It would have hardly mattered if these judgements had been meant as purely personal reactions by practising poets (whose right to grind their own little individual axes one cheerfully concedes), but the matter assumes an alarming significance when such rash verdicts are seriously offered as criticism.

In fact, the current fashion to turn up one's (not necessarily Aryan) nose at all pre-Independence Indian English poetry because it is by and large romantic shows a shocking ignorance of the entire Indian literary tradition, which goes back to millenia. The revolt against romanticism by T.S. Eliot, Ezra Pound and T.E. Hulme had, as pointed out earlier, its own justification in the context of Anglo-American poetry, but in echoing the Western master's voice, it never struck us to ponder its total validity in the immediate context of Indian literature at all. The fact is that the Indian literary tradition, right from its beginning in ancient Sanskrit literature, has always been predominantly 'romantic.'

It is, of course, extremely difficult to define precisely terms like 'romantic' and 'romanticism,' there being perhaps as many definitions as there are critics and philosophers. In his *The Decline and Fall of the Romantic Ideal* (1954), F.L. Lucas noted that there were 11,396 books on Romanticism.[9] But that was more than four decades ago, and the number must have swollen inordinately during these years. Some of the prominent definitions of Romanticism include: a fascination for medievalism; a love of the strange and the exotic; a return to Nature; the revolt against reason; an assertion of Individualism; a liberation of the unconscious; a revival of idealism; an assertion of emotionalism; a thirst for the transcendental, and a passion for artistic experimentation. But all these are perhaps only so many facets of that highly complex phenomenon called Romanticism, which it is manifestly difficult to catch in the net (howsoever capacious) of a single definition. Nevertheless, a precise definition is sometimes a will-o'-the-wisp, as in the case of poetry, for instance. We all know what poetry is, but is a universally acceptable definition at all possible? By the same logic, it is possible to say that we all comprehend the phenomenon that Romanticism is, but can at best offer only a working description of it.

It will be universally agreed that Romanticism is a kind of an art which usually enshrines a world-view shaped by a highly emotional, imaginative and transcendental approach to Reality. This description certainly fits a large part of ancient Sanskrit creative literature, a work which is mostly in the realistic vein being an exception. The Persian influence which came to be felt after the Muslim conquest of India during the Middle ages, was also predominantly romantic in character and actually strengthened the indigenous romantic tradition. All this naturally resulted in the establishment of certain literary conventions having a clear validity in the total cultural ethos of India over the centuries, which in spite of the strong Western impact from the eighteenth century onwards has maintained an unmistakable continuity and permanence in the midst of manifest and inescapable change.

In addition to this, Indian English literature was an inevitable product of the Indian renaissance of the nineteenth century. It was an age of the rebirth of the Indian spirit after centuries of intellectual and cultural stagnation and the general tone and temper of an age like this could not but make for an art predominantly romantic in spirit, thus strengthening further a tradition which had already been established firmly over millennia.

In fact, there was a vital point of difference between the reception of Romanticism in post-World War Britain and India of the same period. In the light of the economic depression and general disillusion of the nineteen twenties in Britain, Romanticism naturally began to appear an outmoded world-view. But the rigours of War were never felt in India to the same extent then. On the other hand, the Gandhian movement, which had begun to galvanise the entire country, had ushered in a new era of dedication to the intensified freedom struggle—an era of vigorous political activity and hope. "Thode din me Gandhiraj" (We will have the rule of Gandhi within a few days) was the slogan of the times. It is no wonder that an age like this found kindred spirits in the British romantic poets.

Actually, the situation continued to be very much the same until the attainment of freedom in 1947. The tempo of the freedom struggle was intensified further after the Quit India movement was launched in 1942. The rigours of the second World War and its equally terrible aftermath in Britain have therefore no parallel in the India of the day. Romanticism still remained a potent influence. A tell-tale example of this is the poetry of Kusumagraj in Marathi. During the nineteen forties, he wrote verse fired by the spirit of revolution ('Roar Victory to Revolution, roar victory' is perhaps his best-known poem) and his accents are completely authentic. This poetry is no carbon copy of the work of Shelley and Byron, but an art which has lighted its torch at the age-old fire of Romanticism. This can be said of the best poetry of Sri Aurobindo, Tagore and Sarojini Naidu also. Practically unaffected by the two

World Wars, they pursued their own Indian concerns, in typically Indian ways.

This has naturally led to their being much misunderstood by western critics. A common charge against Sarojini Naidu and Tagore, for instance, is that of sentimentality—a charge which we in India have dutifully endorsed in our zeal to echo the master's voice. But the uninhibited expression of emotion has not only been an age-old Indian literary convention, but like all such conventions it also has its roots in the cultural ethos of the land. The Indian personality does not fight shy of open expression of emotion and even today in certain parts of India the employment of professional mourners is one of the accepted ways of showing customary respect to the dead. It is therefore not difficult to understand why Bhavabhuti, one of the greatest of ancient Indian dramatists, declared that pathos was the only rasa (in western aesthetics, the tragic is superior to the pathetic) and why, as H.W. Wells[10] has noted, swooning is actually a well-established convention in ancient Sanskrit drama, there being as many as sixteen episodes of characters fainting with excess of emotion in *Uttararamacharita* alone. Apart from this play, all the other prominent examples of pathos in ancient Sanskrit literature viz. Bhasa's *Urubhanga* and *Karnabhara* and the three Kalidasian laments—those of the mad Pururavas in *Vikramorvasiya*, Rati in *Kumarasambhava* and Aja in *Raghuvansa* (not to mention many passages in the *Ramayana* and the *Mahabharata*) are marked by a patently stylized expression of grief, deliberately couched in decorative terms, with free use of simile, metaphor and other poetic figures. To dismiss these passages as artificial and sentimental is to display crass ignorance of the literary and cultural tradition to which they belong. Surely, what appears to be sentimental to the stiff-upper-lipped Englishman (one recalls E.M. Forster's well-known complaint against the "under-developed heart" of the British) need not necessarily seem to be so to those who have their roots in another way of life.

Another charge often levelled at Indian writers in general and the Indian Romantics in particular is that of ornateness. "Magniloquent," "grandiloquent," "over-decorative" and "lush" are some of the adjectives routinely used in describing Indian style. Here again, it is important to remember the vital connection between style and both the Man and the Milieu. It is hardly surprising that in a land which provides an astonishing variety of climate, scene and setting, and where nature sports an unimaginably varied display of vivid colour almost throughout the year, decorativeness should be a value firmly rooted in popular experience. It is equally obvious that this would appear to be merely exotic to British eyes normally used to pea-soup, fog weather and dull, grey skies.

In his essay on "Wordsworth in the Tropics,"[11] Aldous Huxley has argued convincingly that this poet's entire attitude to nature would have been far different had he lived in the tropics. Surely, the same logic should apply to a poet's aesthetics also. Ornamentation has always been an important value in the Indian literary tradition.

Agnipurana, which contains probably the earliest aesthetic thinking of the Hindus, declares, "Poetry without figures of sense is like a widow."[12] Jayadeva avers, "A man who agrees that there can be poetry without figures of speech is capable of maintaining that there can be fire without heat"[13]; and Kuntaka states that "the adornment and the adorned . . . together constitutes poetry."[14] The general ornateness of Sanskrit style was a natural result of these attitudes.

This according of a high place to ornamentation in art probably made the ancient Hindus see no distinction between 'fine' and 'useful' arts, so that even a practitioner of a useful art was supposed to display his aesthetic sense in his creation. The extreme limit to which this principle was stretched is illustrated in Sudraka's play, *Mricchakatika* (Act III), where Sarvilaka, the burglar, takes pride in showing his artistic still in making an elegant hole in the wall, while burglaring Charudatta's house.

This cult of ornamentation was further strengthened under the Persian influence after the Muslim conquest, and made for the courtly style with its high-flown flourishes, of which a letter written by the Sikh king, Ranjit Singh to the British Governor-general is a typical specimen. The king tells his correspondent: "Friendship was refreshed with a fragrant drop of dew. It gave me delight as the rose-petal in the beak of the bulbul on the dawn of accomplished hopes."[15] We do not, of course, speak in this strain any longer, but its influence has gone very deep into our culture. Thus, the pedestrian question, "May I know your name?" is put in Hindi as "May I know your good name?" and in Urdu, there are as many as eleven forms of polite address beginning with "'Janab' (Sir) and rising progressively with gradation such as 'Janab-e-vala' (Honourable Sir) and 'Janab-e-Ali' (exalted Sir), 'Sarkar' (Master) upto 'Quibla-e-Kaba' (Your Holiness)."

It is thus high time we ceased to look at Indian Romanticism through western blinkers, and learned to relate it firmly to our indigenous traditions. It is only then that we shall be able to evaluate it properly. It is, of course, true that when the major Indian romantic poets were writing, there was a lot of putatively romantic verse also being written, which was a pale imitation of British romantic, Victorian and Georgian poetry. There were perhaps far too many would-be Wordsworths and Babu Byrons, Shelleys in sherwanis and community Keatses. But in discarding all this chaff, let us not neglect the golden grain underneath.

Further evidence for recognizing the vital importance of Romanticism in the Indian literary situation is discovered when one turns from Indian English literature to literatures in the modern Indian languages. Curiously enough, in many of these literatures, the 'new' poetry drew its inspiration from the great British romantics. For Keshavsut (1866-1905) the pioneer of modern Marathi poetry and his contemporaries like Tambe and others, Palgrave's *The Golden Treasury* became a variable poetic Bible. In fact, the romantic influence continued to remain strong in Marathi poetry right upto the nineteen forties. Similarly, in Kannada, B.M. Srikataiah's *Inglish Gitagalu* (Songs from English, 1921) marks a turning point in modern Kannada verse, and most of the lyrics translated by Srikantaiah were those by the British romantics. And in modern Assamese literature, the renaissance began, when the monthly *Jonaki*, which ushered in the romantic movement, was founded by Laxminarayan Bezbarua (1867-1938) and others.

Let us therefore not denigrade blindly Romanticism, by echoing some western opinion; for the Romantic world-view and Romantic art did not begin with the British Romantic poets; they are as old as literature itself and will live as long as literature survives.

NOTES

1. W.W. Robson, "A Poet's Notebook: The Use of Poetry and the Use of Criticism," *The Literary Criticism of T.S. Eliot*, ed. David Newton-De Molina (London: The Athlon Press, 1977), pp. 152-53.
2. F.R. Leavis, "Literary Criticism and Philosophy," *The Common Pursuit* (Harmondswoth: Penguin Books, 1962), p. 221.
3. Qtd. F.R. Leavis, *The Common Pursuit*, p. 38.
4. R. Parthasarathy, *Ten Twentieth Century Poets*, Introduction (Delhi: OUP, 1976), p. 3.
5. P. Lal and K. Raghavendra Rao, *Modern Indo-Anglian Poetry: An Anthology*, introduction (New Delhi: A. Chaya Devi, 1959), pp. iii-v.
6. Nissim Ezekiel, "Replies to the Questionnaire," *Modern Indo-Anglian Poetry: An Anthology and a Credo,* ed. P. Lal and K. Raghavendra Rao (Calcutta: Writers Workshop), p. 169.
7. K.N. Daruwalla, "Replies to the Questionnaire," *Modern Indo-Anglian Poetry: An Anthology and a Credo*, p. 94.
8. K.N. Daruwalla, Introduction, *Two Decades of Indian Poetry*, 1960-1980 (New Delhi: Vikas), pp. xxxiv-xv.
9. F.L. Lucas, *The Decline and Fall of the Romantic Ideal* (Cambridge: Cambridge University Press, 1954), p. 3.
10. H.W. Wells, *The Classical Drama of India* (Bombay, 1963), p. 87.
11. Aldous Huxley, "Wordsworth in the Tropics," *Do What You Will* (London, 1936), pp. 90-103.
12. *Agnipurana*, Chapter 344, verse 2 (Poona, 1900), p. 430.
13. Jayadeva, *Candraloka*, ed. Pandit A.R. Vetal, I, 8 (Benaras, 1938), p. 4.
14. Kuntaka, *Vakroktijivita*, ed. K. Krishnamoorthy, I, 6 (Dharwad, 1977), p. 6.
15. Khushwant Singh, *Ranjit Singh* (New Delhi, 1968), p. 138.

Is This What Romanticism Has Done?

VIVEKANAND D. PHADKE

Lilian R. Furst begins her monograph on *Romanticism* in the Critical Idiom Series with E.B. Burgum's warning in 1941: "He who seeks to define Romanticism is entering a hazardous occupation which has claimed many victims."[1] She goes on to mention that in 1924 Lovejoy had said "The word 'Romantic' has come to mean so many things that, by itself, it means nothing."[2] Perhaps that's why he has used a plural noun—Romanticisms—in the title of his essay.

One of these Romanticisms, represented by William Godwin, is 'revolutionary' in spirit. Even before Wordsworth and Coleridge published their *Lyrical Ballads*, Godwin had published his *Enquiry Concerning Political Justice* in 1793 in which he made his trend-setter argument: "Government is the perpetual enemy of change. . . . They 'lay their hand on the spring there is in the society, and put a stop to its motion.' Their tendency is to perpetuate abuse. . . . By its very nature positive institution has a tendency to suspend the elasticity and progress of mind, . . . since government, even in its best state, is an evil, . . . We should have as little of it as the general peace of human society will permit."[3]

Godwin extended his idea that any kind of authority is against nature and breeds social evils to other concepts like property and marriage beyond the political field. Property, according to him, is a source of power over others and by "the evil of marriage," men and women are "reduced to make the best of an irretrievable mistake." (Book VIII, Chap. VIII)

After Godwin, the revolutionary spirit awakened by Romanticism was developed by Pierre-Joseph Proudhon around 1840 through *What is Property?, Economic Contradictions, The Federal Principle, The Political Capabilities of Working Class. Egalitarianism*, decentralized federalism and direct action were the essential doctrines taught by him. In 1864, his followers founded the First International. From Proudhon, the baton of Anarchism was handed over to Mikhail Bakunin, who replaced Proudhon's individualism and non-violent method by collectivism and by violent action. He said: "The passion for destruction is also a creative urge."[4] After Bakunin's death in 1876, the mantle of theoretician of Anarchism fell on Peter Prince Kropotkin, who visualized a Utopia of a revolutionary society as a federation of free communist groups.

We find the emphasis shifted from theoretical writings to the insurrectionary deed as the most efficacious means of propaganda after Prince Kropotkin. The first insurrections were rural uprisings, but, when they were ruthlessly crushed, they took the form of individual or group deeds of protest by terrorists. Modern urban/political terrorism thus appeared on the horizons of human civilization.

How did Romanticism relate to this evolution of revolutionary spirit from Godwin to Baader-Meinhof?

The major Romantics were influenced by Godwin's ideas. Godwin was once heralded as the prophet of revolutionary spirit in England, though his ideas were later repudiated by the Romantics. Shelley praised the "tempestuous loveliness of terror" and *Queen Mab and Revolt of Islam* were defiantly anarchist poems. It is as if Bakunin is only paraphrasing "Ode to the West Wind." Oscar Wilde declared himself an Anarchist and, inspired by Kropotkin's ideas, wrote his essay, "The Soul of Man under Socialism." Avant-garde painter like Courbet regarded Proudhon as his master. As late as 1946, we find Aldous Huxley asserting in his Foreword to the new edition of *Brave New World* that only by radical decentralization, simplification and a Kropotkinesque, co-operative politics could the dangers before modern society be avoided.

Just as Romanticism had endorsed, upheld and thereby legitimized Godwin's anarchism, its descendent manifestations like symbolism, surrealism, modernism were deeply sympathetic to radicalism and syndicalism. Therefore, one line of cultural criticism, represented by Irving Babitt and Mario Praz, castigates Romanticism as a pernicious bane. According to them, it opens a Pandora's box hoping or feigning to find something like elixir. However, what is unleashed is, among other things, something monstrous, that which needs to be tightly bottled by the classical virtues of Rationality, Intellect and Restraint.

How did this metamorphosis of sublime intentions into 'sinister' effects take place? There seem to be three processes operating. One is the commonly observable phenomenon that when the control of a genius propounding a 'revolutionary' concept is gone, its once responsible realizations degenerate into irresponsible caricatures after him. Second is the inevitable and universal blending of the forms of any movement with currents fashionable at times, e.g. blending of Romanticism with Leninism, mystics, religiosity, idealism, adventurism, fanaticism, apocalypsism, mania, obsessions and just crude arrogance. The resultant brew—terrorism—is quite toxic.

The third process is more complex. During the course of time, one single strand is isolated from what is actually a closely interloping yarn of concepts. In the second stage, this strand is given disproportionate importance. As Hazlitt said of Godwin in *The Spirit of the Age* in 1825: "Mr. Godwin's theory, and that of more approved reasoners, differ only in this, that what are with them the exceptions, the extreme cases, he makes the every-day rule."[5]

In the third phase, this isolated, now-concentrated concept gets transformed into something other than itself, something entirely unexpected, especially if coupled with other options on the way.

Does this mean that Romanticism is responsible, directly or indirectly, for PLO, Red Army, or closer home, for People's War Group? Is this what Romanticism has done?

It must be conceded, gleefully by some, usefully by others, that it has at least contributed, may be unintentionally, to the general climate in which anarchism/radicalism realized into darker, negative manifestations of human imagination in the fields of arts as well as politics. Their simultaneous existence is fairly obvious; causality is a matter of debate. To quote Hazlitt again, "The fault of Mr. Godwin's philosophy, in one word, was too much ambition—by that sin fell the angels! He raised the standard of morality above the reach of humanity and by directing virtue to the most airy . . . heights, made her path dangerous, solitary and impracticable." No wonder his ideas disintegrated and degenerated.

NOTES

1. Lilian R. Furst, *Romanticism* (London: Methuen, 1969), p. 10.
2. Lovejoy, "On the Discrimination of Romanticisms," *PMLA*, 39 (1924), pp. 229-53.
3. William Godwin, *Enquiry Concerning Political Justice* (1793), Chap. VII, BOOK III.
4. *Encyclopedia Britannica*, Vol. 2, p. 809.
5. William Hazlitt, "William Godwin" in *The Spirit of the Age* (1825).

Keats's Theory of Poetry and Eliot's Theory of Impersonality

K.S. IYER

It is my contention that Keats's theory of poetry, as it emerges from his letters and as demonstrated in "Ode to a Nightingale," needs to be examined vis-a-vis Eliot's Theory of Impersonality. Such an examination will reveal that Keats, in several ways, was a forerunner since he, too, considered a poem to be a composition in a state of "a complete disinterestedness of mind."[1] A few statements made by Eliot in his essay "Tradition and the Individual Talent" should serve as "premises" for such an examination of Keats's theory of poetry and its application to the ode in question.

1. The progress of an artist is a continual self-sacrifice, a continual extinction of personality.
2. The poet has no personality to express, but a particular medium.
3. A poem is a combination of several emotions, ideas, phrases and images, which clamour for inclusion in it.
4. Poetry is not inspiration, but intuition, intensity and concentration.
5. The more perfect the artist, the more completely separate in him will be the man who suffers and the mind which creates.
6. Poetry is not a turning loose of emotions, but an escape from emotions.

Now, to turn to Keats's Theory of Poetry. In letter No. 31 which Keats wrote to Benjamin Bailey, he exclaims, "Oh! for a life of sensations sweet, rather than of thoughts." By the term "sensations" Keats meant, intuition. Intuition referred to aspiration. Keats wanted 'sweet sensations of truth,' that is real apprehension that transcended notional apprehension. Such an apprehension results when the artist is in a mood of diligent passiveness or passivity. This is Keats's "diligent indolence." In this mood the artist is untouched by pleasure or pain. In letter no. 123 to George and Georgiana Keats, he calls this mood a state of "complete disinterestedness of mind." Keats observed things steadily, to comprehend them in all their concreteness without interposing a philosophic interpretation. He experienced pure delight in the life of nature and in human forms. The life of sweet sensations was later compressed into an image or phrase. This process of experiencing and expressing, he calls "intensity" in another letter. By intensity he meant a passionate and imaginative reaction to an object or event. Such a reaction led him to a sympathetic participation, in which the consciousness of anything other than the object is obliterated. This reaction, for Keats, was so absolute as to make him speak of 'excess' in his letter no. 51 addressed to John Taylor: "I think poetry should surprise by a fine excess, and not by singularity." The word "excess" should be taken to mean, a vivid imaginative concept of the state longed for by the poet. By "excess" Keats also meant the play of all the senses. This leads to the theory of impersonality, whereby the poet gives expression to what the readers feel but fail to articulate. In letter no. 32, written to his brothers, Keats says: "The excellence of every art is its intensity, capable of making all disagreeables evaporate, from their being in close relationship with beauty and truth." Intensity involves an eager yearning for a full, vivid and concrete experience. From the discussion thus far, it is clear that Keats' theory of poetry closely toes the line of the premises 1, 2 and 4 which talk about impersonality, a kind of "disinterestedness" as Keats calls it, and "intuition" and "concentration."

In letter No. 90 written to James Hessey, Keats says: "The genius of poetry must work out its own salvation in a man. It cannot be matured by law and precept, but by sensation and watchfulness. That which is creative must create itself. The sensuous delight must be transformed into a melancholy awareness of the infinity and mystery of the universe." Keats believed that art purified and elevated nature through a gradual refining of the intellectual powers. This ripening gave him a philosophic understanding. By "philosophy" was meant, says Murry, "a comprehension of the mystery of human life." Such a state of mind demanded great suffering. Accordingly, Keats concerned himself with the 'inexorable good of poetic truth.' Poetic truth came to those, he says in *Fall of Hyperion I*, "to whom the miseries of the world/Are misery, and will not let them rest." In letter no. 31, Keats interprets truth to mean the formulation of a moral. Instead of the poetry of delight and escape, he would run after the greatest poetry which alone offers an interpretation of the meaning and value of human life. This relates to premises 3 and 6 in which an escape from emotions is considered the right preparation for poetic composition. In this regard, Keats's view is similar to that of Eliot. For Keats escape from emotions meant a "transformation of sensuous delight" into a "melancholy awareness of the infinity and mystery of the universe." Keats insists on suffering as the foundation for transcendent poetry—poetry that transcends the personal and the sensual.

Keats's theory of poetry enumerated above, has his "concept of beauty" as the second dimension. The problem with Keats was how to reconcile the loveliness of the world with its transience. Transience of beauty gave rise to sad reflections. In "Ode to Melancholy" he makes melancholy and beauty closely related, leading to his interpretation of beauty of nature in terms of human emotions. Intense pleasure cannot be distinguished from numbing pain. Like Beauty, Melancholy is "seen by none" but the poet. Keats believed that the poet has to move from the luxury of sensations to a mood of unhappiness before he apprehends beauty. For him, yearning for beauty was a spiritual passion. He saw the mighty abstract idea of beauty in everything, as he writes to Fanny in letter no. 186: "Seeing things in their pristine purity and beauty, is seeing them in truth." The "Beauty" he discovered in life was his "Truth." The word, 'Truth' for Keats meant 'Reality' alone, opine Garrod and Ridley.[2] Truth is that which has a lasting value, while Beauty is truer than love. His poetry is an intellectual quest for an absolute certainty, for an apprehension of the ultimate truth, as revealed by reality of the world. At this stage reality and truth become synonymous. Keats observes in letter no. 98 written to George and Georgiana Keats: "I never can feel certain of any truth but from a clearer perception of its Beauty."

To turn to Keats's Theory of Negative Capability, which forms the third dimension of his poetic theory. Keats defines it in letter no. 93: "The poetic character is everything and nothing—it has no character—A poet is the most unpoetical of any thing in existence, because *he has no identity.*" The substance of his theory is that the poet should submit to things as they are, without seeking to intellectualise them. This capability arises, says Keats in letter no. 32, "When a man is capable of being in uncertainties, mysteries, doubts, without any irritable reaching after fact and reason." In this state, the poet 'negates' his personality along with the time and space that condition his experiences. He identifies himself with his characters and speaks as they would in normal life. This is an essential aspect of the dramatic tendency, of the power to achieve a sympathetic identification with someone or something dearer to him than *his own self.* This *self-effacement* is the impersonality of great art. There is a difference, however, between the kind of impersonality that was advocated by Keats and Eliot. For Keats, the poet has to embark on his adventure, transforming himself at will into varied forms. This requires not mere awareness, but a diligent indolence which can make the artistic consciousness immanent in the universal experience. As Ridley says: "a poet endowed with this negative capability, need do nothing but remain passive to set his imagination free to wander where it chooses and there are no limits to its range." Keats felt (like Eliot) that there is a state of "unconsciousness" in which great poetry is produced. In his letter no. 15 to Haydon, Keats affirms this: "things which I do half at random are afterwards confirmed by my judgement in a dozen features of propriety." He calls this a good Genius presiding over the poet's mind. This Genius is 'the mind which creates' in a state of unconsciousness divorced as it is from the 'man who suffered.'

Negative capability, thus, arises from a denial of the poet's ego-yearning. Then alone can emerge a new and fresh self. This reawakening of the poetic self is from the immolation of the egocentric self—the self in romantic poetry. This involves for the poet a descent into unconsciousness, the obliteration of the ego and an intense apprehension of the pain and suffering. In this state poetic creation takes place, where disparate feelings and emotions are transmuted into art-emotions. The intensity which exists at this moment of creation is alike to Eliot's "Concentration," not an extension of the emotions, nor their recollection, nor the turning loose of emotions. As Keats writes in letter no. 31: "Men of Genius are great as certain ethereal chemicals operating on the mass of the neutral intellect . . . but they have not any individuality, any determined character." Thus, Keats's Negative Capability as an agency of poetic creation closely follows premise no. 5, namely the separation of the man who suffers from the mind which creates.

Lastly, to draw a brief reference to "Ode to a Nightingale" to see how through stages Keats transmutes materials of experience into art. He sets the stage by a description of his own sensations, his heartache and a painful numbness, about which he wrote to Bailey. The first stanza does not describe mere dejection but a sort of drugged state. This state is maintained by further intoxication in the second stanza. The third stanza is the memory of the speaker's brother's death. It brings out the contrast between his own immediately experienced happiness in the bird's song, his imaginative participation in an untroubled natural life and a less immediate but more enduring sorrow. In the fourth stanza the speaker realizes that the only way of escaping, to share the happiness of the bird is "on the viewless wings of poesy." For Keats, poetry was first of all imagination, that is, imaginative participation in the bird's life and secondly, the actual poem he was writing. This and the next stanza describe the loveliness of the atmosphere, which is nature. The loveliness makes the moment permanent, but not in the sense Keats would have wished. The only way in which the loveliness can be made eternal is to die, at the moment. The sixth stanza describes the poet's longing for death. It suggests the Freudian death-wish—as Graham Hough says—which is the desire of the call to resist the encroachments of outside experience, to remain enclosed in its own contentment. The speaker's desire for death is only the desire to make a happiness, that is transient, last for ever. In the seventh stanza, by a startling transformation, the nightingale becomes a symbol of the artist, and its song a symbol of the art. "Forlorn," the last word of the seventh stanza is used, primarily, in its archaic sense of "utterly lost," thinks Cleanth Brooks.[3] In the last stanza the repeated word, "forlorn" acquires the meaning "pitiable, left desolate." The word recalls Keats the poet who creates foreseeing a poetic immortality to Keats, the man who suffers, foreseeing only sickness and sorrow and an early death.

"Ode to a Nightingale," therefore, encapsulates Keats's theory of poetry, which while being a classical view of poetry in the romantic age, fully anticipates Eliot's theory of impersonality. Keats's three-dimensional approach to poetry affords a re-appraisal of his concept of poetry in the modern context bridging the road between the romantic age and the modern age.

NOTES

1. J.H. Walsh, ed., *Selected Letters and Poems of John Keats* (Chatto and Windus, 1954), letter no. 123.
2. M.R. Ridley, *Keats's Craftsmanship* (Oxford, 1933).
3. Cleanth Brooks, *Modern Poetry and the Tradition* (1939).

The Romantic Metaphysicals

ROBERT PINTO

The modern reader is fascinated by anything new, either in life or in literature. He wants to venture into new frontiers, break new grounds while probing into past history and combining it with his own present experience. His creativity manifests itself in the art of selecting what is best in the East and the West, the Past and the Present, as well as in bringing forth new concepts or expressions of reality which could be either factual, or ideological. We are used to examining the romantic and the metaphysical movements as separate and independent. The question arises: Is it possible to bring about the marriage of these two movements which are a century and half apart? Is it possible to trace the foreshadowing of the latter in the former? Is it possible to think of the romantic metaphysicals?

The term 'metaphysical' is applied generally to the poets of the early seventeenth century which include Donne, Herbert, Carew, Crashaw, Cowley, Marvell and others. Metaphysical poetry is characterized by the prominence of wit, fusion of intellect and emotion, unification of sensibilities, use of far-fetched imagery, hyperbole and conceits, dramatic elements and colloquialism, psychological realism, the prevalence of the religious and mystical note, etc.

In contrast, the romantic movement which spans the late eighteenth century to the middle of the nineteenth century encompasses both the early romantics like Blake, Wordsworth, Coleridge and Southey, and the later romantics, Byron, Shelley and Keats. Romantic poetry is marked by subjectivity, spontaneity, love of nature, supernaturalism, medievalism, a melancholic note, the predominance of imagination and emotion, love of liberty, interest in the lives of common people and their language, a break from set rules, etc.

As one examines both these important movements one is able to discover certain common features. Both movements came into existence as a revolt against contemporary trends and conventions. Donne revolted against the flamboyance and lavishness in much of Elizabethan verse and thus became the pioneer of the metaphysical movement. Similarly, the romantics reacted against the formalism and externalism of the neo-classicists and gave birth to the revival of romanticism. Both movements abound in lyrical poetry which is the expression of the spontaneous overflow of powerful feelings. The element of wit as well as the ratiocination of emotion is found in both the movements. Both are surcharged with the renaissance of wonder as found in nature and in man. There is an effort to see truth and value beyond the external forms of beauty in nature. Both movements focus on life and its conflict and endeavour to reach out to the depths of the human soul.

The techniques of colloquialism and dramatic expression are employed by poets in both the movements for greater intensity and intimacy. In both, the use of imagery, metaphysical conceits, epigrammatic expressions, hyperbole and paradoxes is quite common. The development of theme or an idea in a syllogistic manner already practised by the metaphysicals is also noticeable in the romantics. The 'unification of sensibilities' as discovered by T.S. Eliot in the metaphysicals is also dominant in the romantics. The poets in both the movements try to recreate their experiences in an appealing and orderly manner. One cannot deny the importance of emotion and wit in either of them. The poets of both the movements are craftsmen of their art. Their poetry appeals to the heart as well as to the mind. Consequently one could affirm that there is the foreshadowing of romanticism in the metaphysicals and thus one could think of the romantic metaphysicals.

The claim for the romantic metaphysicals becomes even stronger as we discover what the romantics themselves have said and discovered in the metaphysicals. Coleridge, one of the greatest romantics, used Charles Lamb's copy of Donne's poems to study and scribbled his observations in the margin. Coleridge wrote, "To read Dryden, Pope, &c., you need only count syllables; but to read

Donne you must measure *time*, and discover the time of each word by the sense of passion."[1] "Coleridge was the first" says Hayward, "to point out the purpose and the significance in Donne's metric."[2] Coleridge not only detected passion, but also the dramatic element in Donne's poetry. Referring to the lines "Yet I had rather owner be/ Of thee one hour, than all else ever" from the poem, "A Fever," he comments: "Just and affecting, as *dramatic*; i.e., the outburst of a transient feeling, itself the symbol of a deeper feeling, that would have made *one* hour, *known* to be only one hour or even one year, a perfect hell!" (268) The element of passion which is the ingredient of the romanticism and metaphysicalism is detected by Coleridge. He asserts Donne's poetry is metrical as he comments on the poem, "Song": "This beautiful and perfect poem proves, by its title 'Song,' that all Donne's poems are equally metrical though smoothness be deemed appropriate to songs; but in poems where the writer thinks, and expects the reader to do so, the sense must be understood in order to ascertain the metre." (266)

Coleridge advocated the need to read the poetry aloud. "W.P. Wood noted in his journals a visit to Coleridge on 29 January 1829 when Coleridge read Donne's poetry aloud to the company." (274) The poetry in order to be enjoyed needs to be read aloud to capture its melody which is devised through particular words and sound patterns. Coleridge says, "considering that not one in a thousand of his readers has any notion how its lines are to be read—to the many, five out of six appear anti-metrical." Referring to "Satire III," Coleridge says: "If you would teach a scholar in the highest form how to read, take Donne, and of Donne this satire. When he has learned to read Donne, with all the force and meaning which are involved in the words, then send him to Milton, and he will stalk on like a master, enjoying his walk." (266) Coleridge further comments on "The Canonization": "One of my favourite poems, as late as ten years ago, I used to seek and find out grand lines and fine stanzas; but my delight has been far greater since it has consisted more in tracing the leading thought throu'out the whole. The former is too much like coveting your neighbour's goods, in the latter you merge yourself in the author, you *become He*." (268) Coleridge appreciates Donne's innovations and greatness and pays tribute to him with an epigram:

With Donne, whose muse on dromedary trots,
Wreathe iron pokers into true-love knots,
Rhyme's sturdy cripple, fancy's maze and clue,
Wit's forge and fire-blast, meaning's press and screw. (274)

William Wordsworth, another great romantic poet also recognized the originality of Donne. When Alexander Dyce was preparing an anthology, *Specimens of English Sonnets*, Wordsworth wrote to him in 1833: "The tenth sonnet of Donne, beginning 'Death be not proud,' is so eminently characteristic of his manner, and at the same time so weighty in thought and vigorous in the expression that I would entreat you to insert it, though to modern taste it may be repulsive or quaint and laboured." (355) Commenting on "Aire and Angels," Coleridge wrote: "The first stanza is able, and reminds one of Wordsworth's apparition-poem." (270) Still another romantic poet Robert Southey says: "Both Donne and Ben Jonson, the two authors by whom the metaphysical poetry was brought into vogue, were rugged versifyers.'" (286) In the *Lyrical Ballads*, both Wordsworth and Coleridge make references to metaphysical poetry and its qualities.

There have been periodical eclipses in the popularity of Donne and other metaphysicals in the last four centuries. However, in the last two centuries, there has been a steady rise. At the beginning of the present century, T.S. Eliot published essays on Andrew Marvell, George Herbert and on the metaphysical poetry which whetted curiosity in the metaphysicals and since then there have been several editions of Donne's poems and critical corpus. T.S. Eliot discovered important elements in the metaphysical poetry namely 'the unification of sensibility' and 'A thought to Donne was an experience: it modified its sensibility.' He showed their relevance and use for the modern poetry. These discoveries not only brought him to prominence but also restored the eclipsed glory of the metaphysicals. But prior to the moderns, it was the romantics in the nineteenth century who rediscovered Donne and the other metaphysicals because of certain taste similar to theirs. An attempt to trace the origin or the foreshadowing of the romantic elements in the metaphysicals would help in the better understanding and reassessing of the romantic movement.

One of the important characteristics of romanticism was the love of nature, the desire to know the mysteries of nature and also to discover man's own identity and place in nature. The clarion call of Rousseau 'back to nature' was harkened to by the romantics and they gave expression to it in their verses which appealed to the temper of man plagued by neo-classicism. Romanticism came as a reaction against neo-classicism which laid emphasis on form, perfection and externalism rather than on essence. It was a protest against the evils of pollution, urbanization and industrialisation. The romantics were poet-prophets who foresaw dangers to humanity and harkened to their inner voice and gave expression to it. The romantics turned towards nature as a reaction to neo-classicism and strove to find a remedy for the existing malady, whereas the metaphysicals were drawn towards nature more by the renaissance spirit namely with the desire to know the riches, wealth and beauty hidden in nature. The ultimate aim of both the movements was to enrich man by enabling him to realize himself.

The romantics perceived nature from three different perspectives which are evident from Wordsworth's "Tintern Abbey." The first attitude is that of a boy who moved by impulses runs towards the beauteous form of nature and enjoys it as he wanders among hills, woods and streams. He is delighted by 'glad animal movements.' The second stage is that of an adolescent when there is aesthetic passion for union with nature. He has sensuous relationship with nature in which he is enthralled by 'the mighty world of the eye and the ear.' There is passion for the beauty and mystery of nature. In the third stage the relationship with nature becomes spiritual and intellectual. The feelings of nature include the suffering of mankind, 'the still sad music of humanity.' The consciousness of the spirit has the power to animate and unite all things. Matthew Arnold recognizes the greatness of Wordsworth. He admires Goethe and calls him 'the physician of the iron age' and Byron as the 'thunder roll,' but he manifests the superior power of Wordsworth in awakening the sensibilities of man towards nature which would give him life and everything. Matthew Arnold extols the magic wrought by Wordsworth in the lines in "Memorial Verses":

He spoke, and loosened our heart in tears.
He laid us as we at birth
On cool flowery lap of earth,
Smiles broke from us and we had ease; (47-50)

The metaphysicals also had recourse to nature from different perspectives and found that it gave deeper meaning to their life. Donne says in the poem, "Twicknam Garden":

Blasted with sighs, and surrounded with teares,
Hither I come to seek the spring,
And at mine eyes, and at mine eares,
Receive such balmes, as else cure every thing. (1-4)

Andrew Marvell, another great metaphysical poet, in the longest of his poems, "Upon Appleton House,"[4] utters these words as he watches the leaves trembling in the wind:

What Rome, Greece, Palestine, ere said
I in this light mosaic read,
Thrice happy he who, not mistook,
Hath read in Nature's mystic book. (581-84)

Marvell was familiar with the aspects of the countryside, its trees, birds, streams, sounds and the songs of the birds. He anticipates Wordsworth in preferring the song of the dove to that of the nightingale. While walking he observes "through the hazels thick espy/ The hatching throstle's shining eye" (531-32). He also notices the woodpecker at work. He almost identifies himself with the birds and the plants:

Thus I, easy philosopher,
Among the birds and trees confer;
And little now to make me wants
Or of the fowls, or of the plants,
Give me but wings as they, and I
Straight floating on the air shall fly. (561-66)

Another lyric of Marvell, "The Garden," is full of sensuous imagery and anticipates Keats in his sensuousness.

Like the romantics, the metaphysicals were also keen observers of nature. Donne's eyes fall on simple beings like the flea or the mosquito. In the poem, "The Flea," he describes minutely its action of sucking blood from the lover and the beloved, being swollen with two bloods, becoming a marriage bed and the temple and finally being killed by the beloved. He also uses ordinary things like the pair of compasses in the poem, "Valediction: Forbidding Mourning" to describe the union and dependence of the lover and beloved in spite of their separation. Through these ordinary objects turned into conceits, Donne was able to transpose the reader into the world of imagination. Similarly Wordsworth using simple objects like the daffodils and the cuckoo was able to affect our souls and enable us to have an experience which is beyond sense perception. In the same way Keats chooses the nightingale in his "Ode to a Nightingale," and Shelley the leaf, wave and cloud in his "Ode to the West Wind" to achieve the same effect. Pater says, "Romanticism is strangeness added to beauty." So the principle of making the simple things look extraordinary is common to both the movements.

Imagination which is one of the important characteristics of the romantic movement is also a dominant feature among the metaphysicals. Cazamian says, "The Romantic spirit can be defined as an accentuated predominance of emotional life, provoked or directed by the exercise of imaginative vision, and in its turn stimulating or directing such exercise. Intense emotion coupled with an intense display of imagery, such is the frame of mind which supports and feeds the new literature."[5] Neilson, an American scholar regards romanticism as the predominance of imagination. In Donne's poem, "The Extasie" the souls of the lover and the beloved leave the body for the time being and are lost in a new world where they negotiate with one another like armies before a war:

> Our Soules, (which to advance their state,
> Were gone out,) hung 'twixt her, and mee. (15-16)

Similarly Keats, having travelled with the nightingale into a new world, asks the question at the end of "Ode to a Nightingale":

> Was it a vision, or a waking dream?
> Fled is that music—do I wake or sleep? (79-80)

The romantics resort to different aids to transcend from the real to the imaginative world. Keats would take 'a draught of vintage' or climb 'on the viewless wings of Poesy' or be lost in the sweet melody of the nightingale. Earlier, Donne had found his way through the dream, through death, through blossom, through the intimacy of a marriage bed, the bank of a river or other natural surroundings which created an atmosphere for the intensity of feeling. In such moments the poets cry out like Keats, "My heart aches, and a drowsy numbness pains/ My sense, as though of hemlock I had drunk." Shelley utters his agony, "I fall upon the thorns of life! I bleed!" Donne, few months prior to his death, pleads for mercy from God: "Will Thou forgive that sin where I begun/ . . . . When Thou has done, Thou has not done/ For I have more." Intensity is the hallmark of both the movements. Wordsworth says, "Poetry is the spontaneous overflow of powerful feelings." When man is overwhelmed with powerful feelings, he forgets himself and lives in the other world of imagination.

Subjectivity is another stronghold of both the movements. The romantics are very much influenced by the ideals of liberty, fraternity and equality of the French Revolution. They wanted to be free, both in their thought and expression. They broke from the thraldom of set rules and formalism and expressed themselves freely as the mood or sense dictated. This attitude made room for variety of poetic forms and expressions (no longer bound by the heroic couplet of the neo-classicists). Thus the genius of Keats flowered in the form of odes, that of Shelley in lyrics and that of other romantics in various forms. Two centuries earlier, the metaphysicals also faced a similar situation. The poets of Renaissance were under the spell of Spenserians. Their poetry was clogged with cloyness, velvety expressions and the lavishness of words and imagery. They composed madrigals to please others. Donne revolted against the conventional verse forms of the regular rhythm, the worn-out similes of the Spenserian school and startled his contemporaries in matter and forms of poetry. The other poet who is also equally known for his metrical originality is George Herbert who called Donne a true 'craftsman' in poetry. Thomas Carew, yet another metaphysical, pointing to the inventive spirit of Donne, sings thus in "An Elegie upon the Death of the Dean of Pauls, Dr. John Donne":

> The Muses' garden, with pedantic weeds
> O'erspread, was purged by thee, the lazy seeds
> Of servile imitation thrown away,
> And fresh invention planted. (25-28)

One finds in the metaphysicals a variety of forms. Donne himself had composed sonnets, elegies, verse letters and epigrams. Marvell has to his credit, "An Horatian Ode upon Cromwell's Return from Ireland." George Herbert excels in his divine poems. Thus the inspiration to experiment was drawn by the romantics from the metaphysicals. In the eighteenth century, Lamb and Coleridge studied the earlier neglected poets and found new treasures in them, specially in the metaphysicals whom they tried to emulate.

The romantics, like the metaphysicals, revolted against ornamental language and made use of the common language of the people. Wordsworth in his *Preface to Lyrical Ballads* lays emphasis on the concept that the poetic language should be "the language really used by men." (line 86) The metaphysicals had already practised it much earlier. Jack Dalglish in reference to the metaphysicals says, "Their language is . . . direct, often colloquial, natural, idiomatic and quite free of any such conventional limitations as characterize Augustan or Victorian poetry."[6] He gives the example of Herbert's poetry for vivid naturalness:

> I struck the board, and cry'd, No more.
> I will abroad.
> What? shall I ever sigh and pine?

Jonson said: "Donne for not keeping of accent, deserved hanging"[7] and he further told Drummond that Donne "for not being understood would perish."[8] These prophecies proved false because Jonson had not seen the nuances and colloquialism of Donne which touched the hearts of the people both in his love lyrics as well as in his divine poems. Whereas Eliot considered Donne as "one of the few great reformers and preservers of our tongue."[9] Donne wrote poems in different poetic forms. Metre in his hands became a vehicle for the expression of his emotions and it assumed the forms of jerks or abruptness in many places to suit the speech pattern. F.R. Leavis observes in his *Revaluation*, "In an age when music is for all classes an important part of daily life, when poets are, along with so large a portion of their fellow-countrymen, musicians and write their lyrics to be sung, Donne uses in complete dissociation from music a stanza-form that proclaims the union of poetry and music. The dissociation is positive; utterance, movement, and intonation are those of the talking voice."[10] Another aspect of the colloquialism is conversational element and dramatic realism. Many of Donne's poems open with memorable lines:

For Godsake hold your tongue and let me love,
("The Canonization")

Twice or thrice had I loved thee,
Before I knew thy face or name,
("Aire and Angels")

Busie old foole, unruly Sunne,
Why dost thou thus,
Through windowes, and through curtaines call on us?
("The Sun Rising")

Donne's sudden and colloquial opening in the midst of a pre-conceived dramatic situation immediately captures our attention and we travel with him. David Daiches says, "The opening, both conversational and startling, projects the reader into the poem in a way that is quite new in English poetry; once in the poem, the reader is held by the complex development of the thought which, twisted this way and that, serves to embody rather than to cool the passion."[11] We find similar pattern in the romantics also in the opening lines:

My heart aches, and a drowsy numbness pains
(Keats, "Ode to a Nightingale")

Bright star, would I were steadfast as thou art
(Keats, "Bright Star")
O Goddess! hear these tuneless numbers, wrung
(Keats, "Ode to Psyche")
O wild West Wind, thou breath of Autumn's being,
(Shelley, "Ode to the West Wind")

Thus we find in both the movements there is an evidence of the combination of both the intellect and emotion. The sensation felt in the opening lines is built up through an intellectual process in different ways: (1) Metaphysical conceit which is an extended metaphor. (2) The syllogistic pattern in developing the idea or the theme and presenting it as a whole or unified experience. (3) Selection of the words and their arrangement to suit speech pattern or any other need. Many of the metaphysicals were men of learning. According to Eliot, they "incorporated their erudition into their sensibility: their mode of feeling was directly and freshly altered by their reading and thought." Where other critics had found bare dialectical argument, Eliot saw a fusion of thought and feeling: in his own words, "a direct sensuous apprehension of thought, or a re-creation of thought into feeling."[12]

William Wordsworth considered poetry as 'the spontaneous overflow of powerful feelings' as well as 'emotion recollected in tranquillity.' The act of recollecting emotions and framing them into a particular literary form e.g. lyric, ode etc. would imply an intellectual activity. Hence romantic poetry like metaphysical poetry implies the exercise of both the mind and the heart where the heart feels and conceives and the mind moulds.

The romantics beheld beauty in various forms. For Keats, 'A thing of beauty is a joy for ever.' Metaphysicals also observed beauty in nature, in a woman and much more in the soul's relationship to God. Pater says, "it is the addition of curiosity to this desire of beauty that constitutes the romantic temper."[13] Thus curiosity and beauty are the two prominent elements of romanticism. These are the integral factors of romanticism: one is intellectual and the other is emotional. James Winny says, "Donne felt imaginatively impelled to create. As the colloquial directness of his language gives his poetry the sense of actual happening, and of an immediate contact with reality, so his dialect seems to confirm the impression of solid truth." (102) He continues, "Donne was to be recognised both as a typical Elizabethan in the extravagance of his wit, and as a poet whose work was to be judged not by the irrelevant criterion of metrical form but by its passionate feeling." (52) George Saintsbury in 1896 wrote that "no one with the finest sense of poetry as an art could have left things so formless as some of Donne's poems; but he asserted that for the reader who knew something of human passion 'there is no poet and hardly any writer like Donne.'"[14] Thus the elements of intellect and emotion merge in both the movements.

Donne wanders, like the romantics, into new areas and draws imagery from new geographical discoveries, scientific inventions and other fields and combines them in a new form to give expression to his new experiences and thus he creates a spirit of wonder and discovery in the reader as one travels along with him in his lines. Watts Dunton says, "Romanticism is a Renaissance of wonder." William Godwin also confirms that Donne "is the most deep thinking and philosophical of our poets" and said of him that he is "full of originality, energy and vigour. . . . Every sentence is exclusively his own . . . his thoughts are often in the noblest sense of the word poetical."[15]

The romantic poets continuously turn to nature to find there a truth and value. They lay emphasis on childlike experience which is centred round emotions and feelings. Such thinking finds expression in the poetry of Blake, Wordsworth, Coleridge, Keats, Byron and Shelley. Often we think that the romantics have a positive philosophy or a message based on simple and natural values. Instead, they present conflict, ask questions and reveal the gulf between innocence and experience, the ideal and the real. Any good poem ultimately confirms that "reality is more complex and confusing than any order that the poet might create."[16] The mingling of the real with the unreal, mundane with the spiritual, the transitory with the transcendent is very much present in both the metaphysicals and the romantics. Very often one leads to the other and one can also observe the struggle in the process. The greatest struggle is the conflict between the world of reality and the ideal world. For example Wordsworth begins 'to see meaning into the objects or things of this world.' Keats also sees beauty beyond the ugly reality of suffering and pain in this world. Donne realizing his world of sinfulness asks God for forgiveness, "Wilt Thou forgive that sinne by which I'have wonne/ Others to sinne? and, made my sinne their door?" ("A Hymne to God the Father," 7-8) Thus he decides to live in a world of peace, even before his death, with a certainty of being saved. Wordsworth realized that it is nature and mind working together that can create deep harmony. And a still greater truth was proclaimed when the romantics tried to alleviate the sufferings of mankind following the idea earlier expressed by Donne that 'No Man is an *Iland*, intire of it selfe; every man is a peece of the *Continent*, . . . *Any* Mans *death* diminishes *me*, because I am involved in Mankinde."[17] In a way both the movements strive towards beauty, truth and greater life.

Donne, the pioneer of the metaphysical school of poetry was romantic in his life as well as in his literary works. He was very romantic in his appearance.[18] Referring to his youth, Richard Baker, the biographer, writes that he was "not dissolute but very neat; a great visitor of Ladies, a great frequenter of Playes, a great writer of conceited Verses."[19] His love for Ann More, his beloved, landed him in prison. His adventurous persuasion and perseverance led him to become the royal chaplain and finally the dean of St. Paul's Cathedral. More than the life, his writings were marked by originality in thought and expression. John Carey writes, "Donne's contemporaries recognized him as a totally original and matchless poet. He was 'Copernicus in poetrie': greater than Virgil, Lucan and Tasso put together. Even embittered traditionalists, who found Donne upsetting, acknowledged his revolutionary impetus."[20]

Donne's copernican revolution in poetry not only influenced his contemporaries and the methphysicals but also the romantics as we have already examined. As we are reconsidering romanticism we need to be aware of the trends that are shaping philosophy, psychology, theology and literature of today. We observe a move towards synthesis, unification and globalization. The present century has witnessed an evolution from modernism to post-modernism; structuralism to post-structuralism, yet it lives in the throes to be born in a better and nobler form as a reflection of a whole man. In the past, the ability or genius of a person was judged by his I.Q. but today we also resort to E.Q. Hence both are given prominence. The unification and balance of both is vital for the total personality of an individual as well as of a society. Hence there is a need to combine both intellect and emotion in literature which was earlier represented separately by the metaphysicals and the romantics. Now we need to emphasize neither one nor the other, rather to see them as complimentary. Thus we need to look at romanticism from the perspective of metaphysicals and allow the romantic-metaphysicalism to be born. Is not every person born to be a romantic-metaphysical? Can we call the new trend of unification of intellect and emotion in literature romantic-metaphysicalism?

NOTES

1. "On 2 May 1811 Coleridge scribbled notes in the margin of Charles Lamb's copy of Donne's poems and added a message excusing himself to Lamb: 'I shall die soon, my dear Charles Lamb, and then you will not be vexed that I had bescribbled your book.'" See A.J. Smith, *John Donne: The Critical Heritage* (London: Routeledge & Kegan Paul, 1985), p. 265.
2. John Hayward, *John Donne: A Selection of His Poetry* (England: Penguin, 1950), p. 11.
3. H.J.C. Grierson, *The Poems of John Donne*, 2 vols. (Oxford, 1912). A.J. Smith, *John Donne: The Complete English Poems* (England: Penguin Education, 1973). John Hayward, *John Donne: Complete Poetry and Selected Prose* (London: The Nonesuch Press, 1978). A.C. Patridge, *John Donne: Language and Style* (London: Andre Deutsch, 1978). Helen Gardner, *John Donne: The Divine Poems* (Oxford: Clarendon Press, 1982). John Carey, *John Donne: Life, Mind and Art* (London: Faber and Faber, 1985). Claude J. Summers and Ted-Larry Pebworth, ed., *The Eagle and the Dove: Reassessing John Donne* (Columbia: University of Missouri Press, 1986).
4. "Marvell seems to have spent some two years (1650-52) as tutor to Maria Fairfax at Nun Appleton, the seat of Thomas, Lord Fairfax." See Frank Kermode and Keith Walker, ed., *Andrew Marvell* (Oxford: Oxford University Press, 1994), p. 142.
5. Legouis and Cazamian, *History of English Literature* (New Delhi:

Macmillan India, 1981), p. 997.

6. Jack Dalglish, *Eight Metaphysical Poets* (London: Heinemann, 1967), p. 7.
7. Qtd. in James Winny, *A Preface to Donne* (London: Longman, 1982), p. 48.
8. John Hayward, *John Donne: A Selection of His Poetry* (England: Penguin, 1950), p. 13.
9. Theodore Spencer, *A Garland for John Donne* (Harvard Univ. Press, 1931), p. 19.
10. F.R. Leavis, *Revaluati*on (England: Penguin, 1964), p.18.
11. David Daiches, *A Critical History of English Literature* (New Delhi: Allied, 1994), vol. II, p. 364.
12. James Winney, p. 53.
13. Qtd. in J.N. Mundra & S.C. Mundra, *A History of English Literature*, (Bareilly: Prakash, 1993), vol. II, p. 262.
14. Qtd. in James Winney, p. 52.
15. *The Critical Heritage*, p 19.
16. John Peck and Martin Coyle, *Literary Terms and Criticism* (London: Macmillan, 1993), p. 64.
17. Anthony Raspa, *Devotions upon Emergent Occasions* (Oxford: O.U.P., 1987), p. 87.
18. See James Winney, p. 32 for the Portrait of Donne in a ruff, by Isaak Oliver, 1617. See also the Picture of Donne by an unknown artist on the cover of the book by A.J. Smith, *John Donne: The Complete English Poems* (Penguin, 1973).
19. R.C. Bald, *John Donne: A Life* (Oxford: Clarendon Press, 1986), p. 72.
20. John Carey, *John Donne: Life, Mind and Art* (London: Faber and Faber, 1985), p. 9.

"On *that* side Idolatry": A Re-Appraisal of Romantic Criticism with Special Reference to Shakespeare

PRABHA SAMPATH

The title of my paper derives from Ben Jonson—a distinguished contemporary of Shakespeare and one of the few who could talk of him with objectivity, detachment and yet do justice to his genius. "For I loved the man" confesses rare Ben in his *Timber* or *Discoveries,* "and do honour his memory on this side *idolatry* as much as any . . ." I wonder if Ben Jonson was already able to see how the tide would turn in a hundred years's time. Strange, that he should be the first to use the word *idolatry* with reference to Shakespeare; idolatry would give way to a new coinage exclusively reserved for Shakespeare. Bardolatry—which the Oxford dictionary defines as 'worshipful idolatry of the bard of Avon.'

This paper proposes to examine the contribution of Romantic criticism to bardolatry—and also, what it had to offer, by way of more enduring, constructive nature, to Shakespeare criticism. The underlying assumption here of course is this: How an age looks at Shakespeare, what a particular writer has to say about Shakespeare tells us a lot about that age, and the writer—perhaps it reveals as much about them, as it does about Shakespeare. One of the most valuable lessons that Shakespeare can teach us is to look at criticism objectively; to criticize the critic, if one may be allowed to borrow Eliot's words. In this context, I'd like to quote Shakespeare himself:

Study is like the Heaven's glorious Sun

> That will not be deep search'd with saucy look
> And shall have continual plodders ever won
> Save base authority from others' books.

How people study Shakespeare is therefore of perennial interest.

One point is worth making right away. The Romantic Age did not *initiate* bardolatry. It legitimized, gave critical accreditation to bardolatry. If we look at the chronology of events,[1] we would find that the bard had already been called "sacred" by Samuel Sheppard in 1651, "venerable" by Dryden in 1681, "divine" by Pope in 1737, "immortal" by Dr. Johnson in 1747, and a "God" in Bell's edition of 1774. Shakespeare's works were compared to the Bible, and his omniscience to God's. In 1770, Dr. Paul Hiffernan drew up plans for the most idolatrous venture of them all—an elaborate Temple to the memory of Shakespeare. Thankfully, the Temple was never built. But the fever was spreading beyond the English Channel. In the publications of the first French translations of Shakespeare by Pierre Letourneur, the translator's introduction venerated Shakespeare as "le dieu createur de l'art sublime du theatre"—the divine creator of the sublime art of the Theatre. This introduction went on to import into French language, a strategic anglicism, namely the adjective "romantique." This was in 1776.

This outright worship of a foreign God was to set off shrill protest from Voltaire. But that is not the concern of this paper.

Gibbon tells us that he thought that there were only two ways of criticizing a beautiful passage—(1) by exact anatomy; (2) by idle exclamation or genial encomium. Gibbon gives Longinus the credit for showing him a third, more remarkable way: "He tells us his own feelings upon reading it, and tells them with such energy that he communicates them." This I cite not merely to illustrate the literary genealogy of Romantic Criticism—but also to stress the point that literary criticism becomes here a sort of objective correlative for the subjectivity, emotionalism and strong personal accent that Romantic criticism shared with Romantic poetry.

The Romantics are undeterred by fears of superstitious veneration. In the ecstasy of their admiration they are often apt; to talk and write as if *they* had discovered Shakespeare, and *they alone* can understand him.

In this open flaunting of their idolatry, they make no attempt to conceal their contempt for earlier critics, whose unpardonable fault is that they were not transported to ecstasy—this is what leads Hazlitt to say of Dr. Johnson: "Johnson had no poetry in his soul; he was pedestrian and unperceptive." Coleridge, characteristically generalizes the issue: "That criticism of Shakespeare will alone be genial, which is reverential. The Englishman, who without reverence, a proud and affectionate reverence, can utter the name of William Shakespeare, stands disqualified for the office of the critic."

At its best, Romantic Criticism is intuitive, sympathetic and interpretative—and the Romantics were indeed the first to discover the distinctive merit and the appropriate dramatic relevance of events, characters and situations, that had hitherto been neglected or misunderstood. The Porter scene in *Macbeth* is a case in point—or to give it the title of De Quincey's memorable article: "On the knocking at the Gate in *Macbeth*." Even so perceptive a critic as Coleridge had dismissed this scene as a vulgar interpolation. It was a case of one Romantic scholar stepping in to rectify the solecism of another—De Quincey was the first to point out that the murder of Duncan cuts us off from the normal human world we live in, and reveals a world of evil. Macbeth and Lady Macbeth are transfigured—she is "unsexed" and he has forgotten that he was born of woman. They have been taken out of the region of human things, human purposes and human desires. Then it is that the knocking at the gate commences. To quote De Quincey: "It makes known audibly that the reaction has commenced; the human has made its reflux upon the fiendish; the pulses of life are beginning to beat again." The comment with which this essay opens is illustrative of the Romantic attitude; De Quincey says this scene always produced in him a peculiarly powerful effect that he could never understand—and so for him the moral of the story is "to exhort the reader never to pay any attention to his understanding when it stands in opposition to *any* other faculty of his mind."[2]

When it comes to sensitive appreciation and total emotional response, there is no one to beat the Romantics—and of course Shakespeare was to them *the intuitive creator* who demanded such a response. In one of his letters to John Hamilton Reynolds, Keats quotes Shakespeare's sonnet:

> When lofty trees I see barren of leaves
> Which erst from heat did canopy the herd
> And summer's green all girded up in sheaves,
> Borne on the bier with white and brisly beard.

His comment is both brilliantly illustrative and maddeningly insufficient. He says of Shakespeare, "He has left nothing to say about nothing or anything. Is this to be borne?"[3] Harold Bloom would take that up to talk about the Oedipus complex of the literary world—*The Anxiety of Influence*.

If this illustrates Romantic involvement and enthusiasm it is also typical of Romantic excess—for here the strongly personal opinion is given a universal significance. This is criticism of the *heart* rather than of the *head*.

Romantic sensitivity and appreciation at its best also helped scholars and playgoers of the period to re-discover Shakespeare's contemporaries. To Charles Lamb must go the credit of helping to revive Jacobean Drama, and also the pleasures of Renaissance prose—the writings of Browne, Burton and Fuller. This did much to promote interest in the Elizabethan age as a whole. It was Lamb's immense range of intense reading which enabled him to publish in 1808, one of the most striking anthologies in the annals of literary history *Specimens of the English Dramatic Poets*—a masterpiece of enquiry into what was at that time, a magnificent but neglected subject.

The beginning of Coleridge's Shakespeare Criticism can be traced to a source that might come as a surprise to many of us. In his Essay, *Supplementary to the Lyrical Ballads* (1815), Wordsworth summarizes contemporary European opinion of Shakespeare—the French thought him a buffoon; (Voltaire had been responsible for that damage); the Italians were unable to appreciate him; "the Germans only, of all foreign nations, are approaching towards a knowledge and feeling of what he is." Wordsworth feels their appreciation is in some respects superior to the English who still consider him "a wild irregular genius in whom great faults are compensated by great beauties." How long will it be, he asks, before it is acknowledged that Shakespeare's judgement was equal to his genius?

This was precisely the gap that Samuel Taylor Coleridge set out to fill. He was the first to establish the *organic unity* of the plays, which the neo-classical critics in their zeal for mechanical regularity had failed to perceive. Coleridge found in Shakespeare, the perfect balance between nature and art, genius and judgement, intellect and feeling.

We are talking here about one of the most significant contributions of Romantic Criticism to Shakespeare studies—against the neo-classical concept of Shakespeare as a "wild and irregular genius"[5] and his plays suffering from "barbarous shapelessness and irregularity," Coleridge was the first to point out that the form/order of Shakespeare's plays is not something imposed from *without*, but something that evolves from within.

Coleridge was that rare combination of poet and philosopher whose work marks a new period in the history of Shakespeare Criticism—indeed of literature studies. His tremendous admiration and understanding of Shakespeare informed the development of his critical theory—and this in turn led to greater insight and sensitivity when he came to analyse and discuss the plays. Thus it is fair to remark that his criticism of Shakespeare is both inductive and deductive.

The Romantics brought with them a new wave by way of a hitherto little discussed "psychological" approach to character. Harry Levin observes that Coleridge was the first to use the adjective "psychological" with reference to Criticism. When we think of Coleridge and the "psychological" approach, we think of Hamlet of course. I give below Jonathan Bate's pithy comment on the issue: "The presence of the prince in Renaissance discourse usually indicates that the artist is examining his own *self*. On the other hand, the presence of his *creator* is often indicative of an attempt to 'annihilate' the self."[4]

Thus typically Coleridge can say "I have a smack of Hamlet myself, if I may say so" while Keats remarks, more cautiously, but equally off the mark: "Hamlet was perhaps more like Shakespeare himself, in his common everyday life." Bate cites this as illustration of the fact that the *self* is a central problem of Romanticism.

Talking of Coleridge and Shakespeare, we cannot ignore the problematic and perhaps not fully investigated issue of Coleridge's indebtedness to the Germans—especially to A.W. Schlegel who centred his theory of art around Shakespeare; and to Schelling who put forward his unique theory of the creative process in art. But as Jonathan Bate points out: "The Germans provide theory, and Coleridge its application to Shakespeare." Further, the Germans rarely came down to particulars; it was Coleridge's signal contribution to the history of Shakespeare Criticism to show how particulars, minute details, combined to produce the unified whole that is Shakespeare's drama. No one analyses opening scenes in such detail, as Coleridge has done; no one before him, drew attention to crucial individual words—such as "honest," a key-word in *Othello*, and the "credibilizing effect" of the word "again" in the opening scene of *Hamlet*.

> It may seem a paradox, but I cannot help being of opinion that the plays of Shakespeare are less calculated for performance on a stage, than those of almost any other dramatist whatever. Their distinguishing excellence is a reason that they should be so. There is so much in them, which comes not under the province of acting, with which eye and tone and gesture, have nothing to do.[5]

It was Charles Lamb who made this paradoxical, aggressively unorthodox statement in the essay with the telltale title: "On the tragedies of Shakespeare, considered with reference to their fitness for Stage Representation." This has elicited the sharpest criticism from later critics who point out that Shakespeare wrote primarily for the theatre, and not for scholars in their closets. Lamb, Hazlitt and Leigh Hunt chose to ignore the obvious, and put forward instead the notion of "the theatre of the mind" where readers could produce, direct and stage their own Shakespeare performances—ideal, abstract and near perfect, to each one as he pleases. We can see how fatally attractive this notion can be, especially to Indian readers for whom access to Shakespeare's stage is severely limited. But the twentieth century has rejected this attempt to transpose Shakespeare from the stage to the page. The desire of modern critics is to do justice to Shakespeare as a man of the theatre, a popular actor-dramatist writing Elizabethan plays for production in an Elizabethan theatre, as entertainment for an Elizabethan audience.

I would not, despite Lamb's assertion, accuse the Romantic critics wholesale of turning Shakespeare's plays into texts. Lamb himself was an avid theatre goer, and his *Essays of Elia* contain some of the best critiques of contemporary Shakespeare performances. Coleridge too, was aware of the plays as drama, and some of his most astute observations spring from casual reviews of performances. In fact it would be safe to say that performance criticism begins with the Romantic age.

The state of the English theatre of the early nineteenth century was in a large measure responsible for the anti-stage statements from Lamb, Leigh Hunt and Hazlitt. The spectacular element dominated the plays. In the storm-scene of *King Lear,* for instance, thunder, lightning and sheets of rain drowned Shakespeare's poetry. Though the age could boast of great actors like Keane and Kemble and Mrs. Siddons, their style of acting was overtly theatrical.

The distinction between *copy* and *imitation* lay at the heart of Coleridge's view of Shakespeare and the theatre: "Drama is not a copy of Nature, but an *imitation*. 'How Natural!' we say—but the very wonder that furnished the *how* implies that we perceived *art* at the same moment."[6]

Dealing with the controversy about the absence of Unities in Shakespeare's plays, Dr. Johnson had maintained that the audience had always been aware of the illusory nature of the stage action. "Surely he that imagines this, may imagine more" rules the learned Doctor. "Delusion, if delusion be admitted, has no certain limitation . . . the truth is that the spectators are always in their senses, and know, from the first act to the last, that the stage is only a stage, and the players are only players."[7] This is magisterial—but also prosaic and down to earth.

Coleridge's position is far more subtle. The audience at a play is neither deceived, nor wholly undeceived. It is in a state of *illusion*, a complex attitude in part self-willed, in part created by the skill of the playwright and the actors. This state of dramatic illusion, Coleridge says, is analogous to a dream. For sleep suspends both voluntary and comparative power. "The fact is we pass no judgement either way . . . the art of the poet and the actors, and the consent and positive abidance of our own will bring us to this point—we choose to be deceived." This in other words is that "willing suspension of disbelief for the moment" which constitutes not only poetic faith, but also dramatic faith. Thus, his criticism at its best supposes that the audience, the actors and the play, each by itself, is incomplete. The play requires the performance on stage and the response of the audience—its goodwill. The spectator requires for his experience, a unified object. This is dramatic criticism that is both subjective and objective—psychological and introspective, *affective* as the critic examines his own state of mind; but also *formalist,* as he appraises the external structure which causes and promotes this reaction.

Romantic Criticism broke new ground in yet another important direction—it extended the frontiers of Shakespearean biography by first scrutinizing the sonnets and then the plays, for revelations of their creator's mind and soul. In Germany Schiller announced his perception of the chief value of the sonnets—their apparent inspiration by an *actual* friendship and love. Keats's friend Brown was the very first to attempt a sequential reading of the sonnets as a personal revelation. And so began the trend of treating the works as "windows" into the mind and soul of Shakespeare; Emerson would say later "Shakespeare is the only biographer of Shakespeare." And Wordsworth made the classically rash statement about the sonnets: "With this key Shakespeare unlocked his heart." Years later, Browning would respond: "Did he? If so the less Shakespeare he."

To return to the whole business of idolatry with which we started—we can take up the paradox of Shakespeare, was he subjective or objective? M.H. Abrams quotes three distinctively different Romantic verdicts; the first from Schiller—"He is like *God,* not visible in his work"; the second from Schlegel—in Shakespeare's work, "the spirit of the author is the most visible"; and the third from Coleridge—"Shakespeare is the Spinozistic deity—an omnipresent creativeness. . . . Shakespeare's poetry is characterless; that is, it does not reflect the individual Shakespeare"; and he concludes with the awe and reverence that so characterizes Romantic Criticism. "How well do we seem to know Chaucer! How absolutely *nothing* do we know about Shakespeare!"[8]

For every action, there is an equal and opposite reaction. When A.C. Bradley, described as "the last and best of the Romantic school of critics," was making waves with his *Shakespearean Tragedy*; just at the time when his book which carried Romantic assumptions to their logical conclusions was being hailed as the most important volume of Criticism since Coleridge, reaction set in—and how!—with Shaw proclaiming to the world—"Shakespeare is for an afternoon, and not for all time." This is the best one liner I have heard on Shaw's Shakespeare Criticism—Shaw is to Shakespeare what the iconoclast is to the idol. He represents the extreme reaction against encomiastic criticism and the idolatry which he despised. It was Shaw who invented the word for Shakespeare worship—bardolatry—which to him was the equivalent of a four letter word. It was Shaw's lack of superstition which led Middleton Murry to remark that Shaw was a better critic of Shakespeare than Coleridge or Goethe. Shaw himself knew that his attitude was anything but detrimental to Shakespeare. He even claims that he is doing Shakespeare a great favour. In his last review as a drama critic, he wrote: "When I began to write, William was a divinity and a bore. Now he is a fellow creature."

But the lingering effects of Romanticism continued to influence major twentieth century approaches. Adopting a new path-breaking approach to analyse Shakespeare's use of imagery, Caroline Spurgeon nevertheless betrays her Romantic tendencies when she attempts to sum up "Shakespeare the man" as he emerges from her study: "He is indeed himself in many ways in character, what one can only describe as Christ-like; that is, gentle, kindly, honest, brave and true, with deep understanding and quick sympathy for all living things."[9] Where, we might exclaim in exasperation, is the man who wrote *Troilus and Cressida* and "Th' expense of spirit in a waste of shame"?

G. Wilson Knight too, opened up fresh avenues in his search for a general philosophical concept behind Shakespeare's plays. It is not without reason that Rene Wellek classes him among "the new Romantics" of the twentieth century. Wilson Knight rejects criticism, which according to him is a "judgement of vision." What he attempts is "interpretation—a reconstruction of that vision."

Though he set a new trend with his symbolic interpretation of the plays, he ranged himself firmly on the side of Coleridge, Hazlitt and Bradley, who, he said taught him to regard Shakespeare "as a philosophical poet, rather than a man of the stage."

To Gary Taylor, looking back over the whole history of bardolatry, the fact that Shakespeare did not fall with the Bastille, that he was not dethroned from his supremacy by the Revolutionary fervour of the Romantics, is problematic. Taylor quotes Hazlitt: "Nothing that was established, was to be tolerated." Shakespeare was one of those established, who ought to have been intolerable. Shakespeare was a playwright, while the English Romantics achieved their greatness in forms other than drama—in essays, lyrics, lectures and letters. Shakespeare did not die young; he left no fragments; he rarely gives in to despair; he did not leave behind his spiritual autobiography; few of his poetic descriptions are devoted to nature. Further, the Romantics valued originality—and Shakespeare was notorious for his borrowings. He was the last person who could be associated with the stylistic simplicity advocated by Coleridge and Wordsworth. Why was Shakespeare not dethroned? How was it that his cultural supremacy survived, even expanded during a revolutionary period when idols were being replaced all over Europe? Why, in Taylor's words, did Hamlet fail to kill Claudius?

Taylor has the answer too. "Although given the opportunity and the injunction to overthrow the literary past, to make everything natural and new, the Romantics could not take arms against a sea of Shakespeare." Hamlet stabs Polonius, not Claudius. In an act of displacement, rather than confront Shakespeare, the Romantics attacked lesser poets in the vernacular pantheon; they directed their hostility on to the editors, critics and adapters of Shakespeare. Dryden, Pope and Johnson conveniently belonged to both categories of target. Instead of confronting, challenging, deposing Shakespeare—they appropriated him. "Having mistaken him for David, the Romantics rushed to defend Goliath and prided themselves on their part in the victory."[10]

The Romantics initiated a new era of Shakespeare Criticism—if it was impressionistic and individualistic, it nevertheless emphasized the spirit of freedom of enquiry. It proclaimed the sheer joy of reading Shakespeare—the Longinian ecstasy—which had a far reaching impact on all criticism. This ecstasy is almost tangible in the writings of Hazlitt and Coleridge. It was not legislative or judicial; it was least concerned with problems of style, diction and genre. It was creative criticism—in the sense that the critic enters imaginatively into the world of the writer, into his thoughts and feelings. Imagination is emphasized both as the basis of creativity and criticism. It is imagination which produces great works of art; and the critic must be gifted with imagination in order to judge its beauty. Least concerned with issues of morality or didacticism, the Romantics went by Coleridge's dictum: "If poetry instructs, it does so only through pleasure." Also, Romantic Criticism emphasized the study of character, while it largely ignored language and poetry. Its major shortcomings were oversimplification, sweeping generalization, and at times critical shortsightedness. What the Augustans had labelled as wildness and irregularity, the Romantics seized upon as Shakespeare's comprehensiveness and variety—his great virtues. The Romantics celebrated the joy of reading Shakespeare. They helped us to a profound understanding of the bard and they gave us criticism that reads like literature.

NOTES

1. See Louis Marder, *His Exits and His Entrances* (London: John Murray, 1964).
2. In W.T. Andrews, ed., *Critics on Shakespeare* (George Allen and Unwin, 1973; First Indian Reprint 1989), pp. 46-47.
3. *Ibid.*, p. 46.
4. *Shakespeare and the Romantic Imagination* (Oxford: Clarendon Press, 1986), p. 19.
5. See W.T. Andrews, p. 37.
6. See T.M. Raysor, ed., *Coleridge's Shakespeare Criticism* (Oxford, 1960).
7. *Preface to Shakespeare*, 1765. cited in W.T. Andrews.
8. *The Mirror and the Lamp: Romantic Theory and Critical Tradition* (New York, 1953), p. 244.

9. *Shakespeare's Imagery and What It Tells Us* (Cambridge Univ. Press, 1935).
10. *Reinventing Shakespeare—A Cultural History from the Restoration to the Present* (London: Hograth Press, 1989), p. 111ff.

Unknown Modes of Being: Wordsworth's Poetry

ANJALI NERLEKAR

It is difficult to praise Wordsworth in these hard times, especially in India. There is so much of Romantic poetry (and so much of Wordsworth, in the selection of romantic poetry) that is pushed down the throats of readers at every course in every university of the country that one hesitates to praise him for fear of seeming trite. On the other hand, in this age of mania and frustration and disintegration, there is also the danger of appearing passé in publicly acclaiming Wordsworth's optimistic vision. Nevertheless, after two hundred years of the publication of that seminal book, *The Lyrical Ballads*, the book that, many say, changed the course of poetry "as with the might of the waters," one needs to repeat the questions that were asked at the centenary seminar on Wordsworth held at the Cornell and Princeton universities in 1951: "What does Wordsworth actually mean to me? Do I feel myself going back to him continually because he gives the kind of profound stimulus and satisfaction that I want?"[1] And despite our great familiarity with this academically venerated poet, I don't know how categorical a "yes" there would be to the above question. Among the Romantic poets, Shelley is more passionate, Keats more sensual, Byron more exuberant and Coleridge more philosophical. Wordsworth is *not* an easy poet to love.

In this context, there is an interesting story that the attendants at the Dove cottage in Grasmere love to relate to the visitors. Dorothy and William Wordsworth lived here from 1799 to 1806, the period when Wordsworth wrote some of his greatest poems. This cottage used to be "crammed edge-full,"[2] as Dorothy put it, with visitors and friends who frequently stayed over. Considering the fact that Wordsworth was not very rich then and that all the housework was handled by the old maid, Molly Fisher and Dorothy herself, very often the guests were treated to a bowl of "pottage," a hasty oat pudding, for breakfast and evening meal. Charles Lamb, who frequented the house, was too well-bred and well-off to be able to survive these meals. So when he came over, he would lock himself in the study upstairs feigning a lack of appetite, hop out of the large window into the garden below and thence to the local pub to partake a hearty meal there and return via the same route. Critics like Douglas Bush are performing a similar act when they complain of what they think as the attenuated, sweet poetic gruel that Wordsworth serves his readers, claiming that it is irrelevant to modern times: "auto-intoxication [is] . . . alien to us, less realistic and less satisfying."[3]

The attempt here will be to counter this approach and adopt the rather unfashionable view that Wordsworth matters. Not because he affords an opportunity to make some complex critical revelation, but simply because, as Matthew Arnold said a hundred years ago, that in this iron time, Wordsworth made us feel, made us aware of something vital about ourselves.[4]

In one of the unpublished extracts of *The Prelude*, Wordsworth says,

> In weakness we create distinctions, then
> Believe that all our puny boundaries are things
> Which we perceive and not which we have made.

and imagines a world

> In which all beings live
> . . . existing as one mighty whole,
> As indistinguishable as the cloudless East
> At noon is from the cloudless West, when all
> The hemisphere is one cerulean blue.[5]

The impulse behind all Wordsworth's poetry is the attempt to overcome the chasm between beings and levels of existence, be it on the social level where class and race serve to keep people apart or on the philosophical level where the Lockean stance divides the material from the mental.

If we make a list of all the human beings that dot the natural landscape in Wordsworth's poetry, we will see a profusion of people who have, until then, not been at the centre of poetic consciousness or the artistic creation—the old Cumberland beggar, the idiot boy, the solitary reaper, the leech-gatherer, the poor Indian widow, the tramp. Although Wordsworth was certainly not the first to bring in the outcasts of society into poetry, he is definitely one of the few major poets then who made them the subject and the basic impulse of his poetic creation. For example, in *The Prelude*, Book 5, there is an incident where as a student, Wordsworth encounters this strange, uncouth figure of the Arab, a figure that he later realizes is really a mystical element of his imagination. This phantasmal Arab reveals to the poet the sublimity and the awe-inspiring nature of creation and poetry.

Here, Wordsworth extends the boundaries of social and poetical acceptance of subjects by bringing in categories of people who have been, at the most, on the margins of poetic discourse. The democratic impulse that fuelled poets like Wordsworth shows itself not only in the inclusion of the common speech of the day into the hallowed ways of poetic diction, but also in the inclusion of the social reject, the lowly being, the ordinary man into the heart of the poetic exploration of man and society. While this might not really upset the poetic or the social apple-cart by its revolutionary fervour, it at least affords a fresh look at how we structure our lives in society by showing that obsession can sometimes stem out of love, or when madness is seen not as a deviation from the straight and the narrow but as a possible alternative to it. The fact that a decrepit leech-gatherer can reveal to the poet the truth of life in nature and teach him how to overcome his personal and artistic depressions—this is evidence enough of the process of assimilation of what was so far marginal.

A similar exercise is undertaken by the poet when he turns his eyes to the world of natural phenomena. Here too the edges are blurred. the edges of the elements in nature that stand as separate entities. There are numerous images where these elements slip in and out of each other to give a composite picture of a world that is made up of all these and yet is a newfound land. Here is an exemplary verse in this context:

shining water, gathering as it seem'd,
Through every hair-breadth of that field of light,
New pleasure. (*The Prelude*, 1, 578-80)

There is water, field and light in these lines, all contributing to the scene of pleasure; yet, is Wordsworth primarily talking of water or light? The water is shining, every pore of its being is infused with light, the light is as objectively "there," as elemental as a field whose crop is ready to be harvested by water. Every element in this description gives an intrinsic attribute to the other—the light gets the solid reality of a field of harvest, the water gets the immanent glory of light, and the field, the earth becomes a shining presence that combines the fluidity of water and the brilliance of light. The distinctive feature of such a unifying process is of water and land and light is that none of these elements lose their separate entities even as their synthesis is an irradiated presence of nature that is unique to the universe of this poet.

These are the unknown ways of relating to the world that emerge from the known ones. This synthesis of the elements gives a vitality, a certain sense of throbbing life to the inanimate world of nature. The movement of attributes and qualities from one to the other creates a new vital world of nature, an active principle in the outer world that reciprocates the inner life of the sympathetic observer. In fact, the final union on the Wordsworthian scale is that of nature and the human mind, a coming together where the line between the observer and the observed vanishes.

In *The Prelude*, Book 4, Wordsworth talks at length about the summer vacation that he spent in the midst of his favourite hills and lakes. He describes the vivid, inverted image of the world he sees in the water as he leans over the side of a slow moving boat. He

Sees many beauteous sights—weeds, fishes, flowers,
Grots, pebbles, roots of trees, and fancies more,

Yet often is perplexed and cannot part
The shadow from the substance, rocks and sky
Mountains and clouds, reflected in the depth
of the clear flood, from things which there abide
In their true dwelling; now is crossed by a gleam
of his own image, by a sun-beam now,
And wavering motions sent he knows not whence,
Impediments that make his task more sweet. (261-70)

Things belonging to the underworld of the sea and things of the earth and sky coalesce into one creation of the imagination as the young Wordsworth is unable to "part / the shadow from the substance." Every aspect of nature seems to have as much validity of existence as any other; more important, this co-existence of sky, earth and sea is shot through with the radiance of a sun beam and the image of the poet's own self, so that the mountains, the clouds, the flowers, the roots of trees now are transposed to the inner landscape of the poet's mind even as they are part of the phenomenal world.

Thus which is the One and which is the many? the self and the world? the body and the soul? The poetry addresses these divisions and shows how porous the membranes between them can be. One of the purposes of the synthesis of the self and the objective world of nature is to locate what has been the perennial problem of the artist, something that Shakespeare, Milton, Yeats, Eliot all tried to look for in their works—a source of permanence, a continuity for one's soul/ ideas/ existence. Wordsworth succeeds in locating it in the natural course of death and renewal. The self and the natural phenomena, if unified in essence, will be permanent even in their impermanence. They will be imperishable like the "woods decaying, never to be decayed" (*The Prelude*, 6, 625) as Wordsworth describes this revelatory scene of nature in the Simplon Pass. There will be a transitory end but a permanent revival of life in the forests as well as in man when he is one with this phenomenon.

In "A Slumber Did my Spirit Seal," while talking of the death of his beloved Lucy, Wordsworth says in the second stanza:

No motion has she now, no force
She neither hears nor sees;
Rolled round in earth's diurnal course
With rocks and stones and trees.

She is dead, and will never come back as a human being, yet she will be in eternal motion on and around the earth, a part of the very sap of the trees, as permanent and immutable as the rocks of which she has become a part. The terrible anguish, the despair that she is dead co-exists with an inexpressible acceptance of this situation. The poet says, how could my Lucy, the vital, throbbing individual, be part of the hard, unliving rocks and stones? How can she be swung round the earth as a mere object without sensations? However the poet also feels that it is but right that it is so, for she will always be there, she will be in the very atoms of the natural phenomena which have no finite being. The conjoining of nature and self, nature and man, then helps the poet achieve a consolation for the loss he suffers, or man suffers—a promise of continuance of the soul, albeit in another form.

This offers him solace regarding yet another important concern of the poet. In most of his major poems, Wordsworth talks about

The heavy weight of many a weary day
Not mine, and such as were not made for me.
(*The Prelude*, 1, 22-23)

The anguish of the poet regarding the passing of adolescence and the heady joys of the period, the frustration of being imprisoned in the world's ways of "getting and spending," find a balm in this union of the soul of nature and man, for it creates a battlement against time and decay in his own person. When Wordsworth revisits the Tintern Abbey, he realizes that his days of glad animal passion in nature are over and there is the anxious question whether he has lost something forever. But this initial sensory coming-together of the boy and nature leaves its vestiges. As he puts it,

the soul,
Remembering how she felt, but what she felt

Remembering not, retains an obscure sense
Of possible sublimity, whereto
With growing faculties she doth aspire
With faculties still growing, feeling still
That whatsoever point they gain, they yet
Have something to pursue. (*The Prelude*, 2, 315-22)

The promise of "possible sublimity" is pursued by man's self because he has had this visionary experience earlier on, and is consequently reassured that it is possible again, although in different contexts. The past and the present, the days "disowned by memory" and the actual instant get connected by this potential for revelatory experiences. The friendship of the elements and man, then, helps the poet to bind his life together, make one whole of his past and present selves and hold out a similar promise for the future.

What is extremely significant is that this transcendence of demarcations takes place not only on the level of life and death or the past and the present, not only on the aesthetic or the metaphysical front, but also on the level of sensation and feeling, space and time. For example, when he describes the lasting feeling of joy that the scene leaves in his mind, he says:

oh, then, the calm
And dead still water lay upon my mind
Even with the weight of pleasure, and the sky
Never before so beautiful, sank down
Into my heart, and held me like a dream!
(*The Prelude*, 2, 170-74)

The water passes on to the realms of the soul to lay its significance on man, and pleasure has a 'weight' as objective and tangible as the water, the sky glides into the heart as though the route from the outside to the inside was smooth and unfenced. What Wordsworth feels is described in terms of physical and external attributes while what he senses—the sky, the water—become a 'dream.' Hence W.J. Harvey's observation that in Wordsworth "place becomes a projection of the psyche"[6] because it is connected with the passage of time and memory. The philosophical rent created by Lockean theories of life in the universe or the psychological chasm that Wordsworth personally experienced between his past and present beings are overcome by the poet by this communion between the world and the self.

Another interesting aspect of this treatment of 'time' is that the events that bob up in memory are not necessarily pleasant. When one goes through the 'spots of time' in *The Prelude* or a poem like "Resolution and Independence" one is forced to conclude that many of the experiences that Wordsworth describes as nourishment to his soul, experiences that have left an indelible mark on his mind, are those that have an element of fear, strangeness, an inexplicable sense of foreboding in them. The peak that seems to pursue the young Wordsworth in Ullswater as he rowed back in terror, the image of the dead body surfacing on the water, the old leech-gatherer who seems almost a sea-beast that has come out to sun itself on the rock—these images indicate that what went into the making of the Wordsworthian soul was not all shining water and moving mists. Nature is bleak, and terrifying even as it is overfull with magnificence, and for the poet, both these contraries go into the creation of his identity. Qualitative distinctions of experiences as good or bad become irrelevant in such poetry, for it is about the fact that:

> all
> the terrors, pains, and early miseries,
> Regrets, vexations, lassitudes interfused
> Within my mind, should e'er have borne a part,
> And that needful part, in making up
> The calm existence that is mine when I
> Am worthy of myself. (*The Prelude*, 2, 344-50)

This self-conscious look at the construction of the human mind, the quest for identity that encompasses the contradictions between the past and the present selves, the good and the solemn experiences of life, and the triumphant proclamation—"when I /am worthy of myself"—thus am I, a sentient and self-conscious man in nature: this reminds me of that famous metaphor from the *Mundak Upanishad*, which could perhaps encapsulate the complexity and the beauty of Wordsworth's poetry for me.[7] In this upanishad, there is the image of a full-grown tree, bounteous and sensual, and there are two birds perched on the branches of this tree. One is eating the fruit of the tree while the other bird is watching, observing, not the tree but the first bird that is enjoying the physicality of the tree. In the upanishad, the world is like the tree while the eating bird is "jeev" and the observing bird is "saakshin." Both the birds together make man. Thus the being who is immersed in the sensual physicality of the world, the doer, if you will, and the being that stands back and observes, analyses—the instinct and the self-consciousness together make the complex being of man.

Wordsworth says as much when he acknowledges the gaps, 'vacancies' as he calls them, in his existence even while he overcomes them in his work:

> The vacancy between me and those days
> Which yet have such self-presence in my mind
> That sometimes, when I think of them, I seem
> Two consciousnesses, conscious of myself
> And of some other being. (*The Prelude*, 2, 29-33)

This complexity, this pervasive look at the construction of the human self is what is so remarkable about Wordsworth's poetry. Thence comes his poetry, a spontaneous overflow of powerful feelings as well as emotions recollected in tranquillity.

Through all this exercise of building bridges across apparent chasms in one's thoughts or one's existences, Wordsworth's poetry conveys a sense of continuity, of beings flowing one from the other, of ideas and emotions that can transcend time and space. One comes away from his poetry with the conviction that this being-in-the-world is more interpenetrating, more inclusive than one could have ever imagined. It bespeaks of a wholeness of body and mind, a fruitful commerce of mind and nature, and says, along with that other extremely physical yet self-conscious poet, John Donne: No man is an island.

NOTES

1. Douglas Bush, "Wordsworth: A Minority Report," in *Wordsworth: Centenary Studies Presented at Cornell and Princeton Universities*, ed. Gilbert Dunkling (New Jersey: Princeton Univ. Press, 1951), p. 8.
2. Nancy Martin, *William and Dorothy Wordsworth at Dove College* (Cumbria: Badger Press; A Wordsworth Trust publication), p. 6.
3. Douglas Bush, "Wordsworth: A Minority Report," p. 15.
4. Lionel Trilling, "Wordsworth and the Iron Time," in *Wordsworth: Centenary Studies*, p. 146.
5. Quoted in Helen Derbyshire, "Wordsworth's Prelude," *The Nineteenth Century*, XCIX (May 1926), pp. 718-31.
6. W.J. Harvey, "Vision and Medium in *The Prelude*," in *Wordsworth: The Prelude*, ed. W.J. Harvey and Richard Gravil (London and Basingstoke: Macmillan, 1972), p. 232.
7. This image was pointed out to me by Archana Degaonkar in a discussion on the Upanishads.

Wordsworth Reconsidered as Romantic Critic and Poet

A.T. KENGHE

One of the ways of distinguishing between classicism and romanticism in theory and practice is to contrast them using common terms in political science such as democratic and antidemocratic. One may easily remember T.S. Eliot's statement about himself that he was a classicist, royalist and Roman Catholic. Though Yeats was influenced by some Romantic poets in some of his poems, his major poetry was classical in spirit as well as in style. That is, he had a stronger interest in the minority of a privileged class rather than in the majority. The antiromantic tradition in modern poetry has on the one hand less concern for the individual liberty of the artist—he must be aware of 'tradition' while showing his 'individual talent'—and on the other, the artist also seems to be indifferent to the majority of the 'ordinary' readers. It is in this sense that classicism may seem antidemocratic.

Wordsworth as critic and poet was more interested in the majority of ordinary readers. The common man, the rustic, was more important to him than the privileged man of the urban civilization. Ordinary people—like the leech-gatherer, the solitary reaper, Susan, and many others—are at the centre of many of his poems. To him they were more natural and less hypocritical in their behaviour, unlike the people dwelling in cities, the people haunted by the ghost of so-called civilization. Besides, Wordsworth's observation of ordinary people made him aware of their extraordinary virtues—for example, courage in adversity of the leech-gatherer and the sweetness of the reaper's song.

As a critic Wordsworth also insisted on the language of common people because, according to him, their language is natural. It expresses natural feelings and experiences and has nothing showy about it. Ordinary people are frank. They do not care to cover the reality by the elegance of civilization. Similarly their language is not calculated to produce a particular effect. Rhetoric is not a recurring characteristic of ordinary people's language. This feeling must have made Wordsworth use ordinary people's language in his poetry.

Classical critics before Wordsworth insisted on a different variety of language for poetry. Ordinary language was not acceptable to them. The classical art is not for the majority, but for a minority of high class.

Classical critics are not in favour of the artist's autonomy. They try to control the artist. They do not believe in the idea of a poet, as Shelley says, like a nightingale singing in darkness.[1] The classical artist is like a singer trying to please an audience, and not like Wordsworth's solitary reaper, who was singing alone without bearing any audience in mind. If individual autonomy or liberty is a mark of democracy, romantic art is democratic in this sense.

Wordsworth is a more democratic critic than Coleridge or Shelley in his concept of a poet, though they are also romantic critics. Coleridge's description of a poet at the end of 'Kubla Khan' suggests the idea of a poet who is almost a superhuman being who has drunk the milk of paradise. He is endowed with the secondary imagination denied to ordinary men. Shelley calls poets 'the unacknowledged legislators of the world,'[2] that is, poets are believed to be extraordinary people.

Wordsworth denies this higher rank to poets. He thinks that a poet is a 'man' speaking to 'men.' This awareness of poet as a man like ordinary men (with some qualities in higher degree) makes Wordsworth a critic more democratic than other Romantic critics like Coleridge and Shelley, though romantic theory of art itself seems democratic in its willingness to grant autonomy to the individual artist.

Classicism emphasizes artistic restraint, and romanticism encourages artist's autonomy. Though Wordsworth rebelled against the classical critics' tyranny, he believed in the artist's internal or mental self-restraint. He called poetry a spontaneous overflow of powerful feelings but elaborated his statement slightly or considerably by adding that it takes its origin in emotion recollected in tranquillity. He did not think of writing a poem immediately at the time of, or after, the intensely felt emotional experience. His act of poetic composition involved a few stages such as that of passing some time, after that remembering that experience, then re-experiencing the re-collected emotion. The probable reason for this was that the value of an emotional experience for others may be determined only by the test of time. If the emotional experience is easily forgotten, then it is not likely to be shared by others. But if it is remembered after a gap of time to the extent of re-experiencing, then it may be worthy of others's notice and pleasure. Another reason why Wordsworth did not think of composing a poem immediately after an emotional experience could be the desire for self-restraint—that is, though any one would be tempted to write a poem immediately after or during an emotional experience, Wordsworth avoided that temptation. It may be noted that this self-restraint is essentially classical.

Wordsworth's feeling of a need for self-restraint on the part of the poet can also be seen in one of the reasons he gives for his choice of verse instead of prose. He believes that verse involves consideration of some definite laws, and such consideration may restrain the poet from being carried away by the intensity of the emotion.[3] Thus though Wordsworth rebelled against the external control of classical critics, he took care of the artist's own self-control. This concern for the poet's self-restraint seems to bring in an element of classicism in Wordsworth's theory of poetry, though he was a romantic critic.

Some classical element may also be noted in Wordsworth's views on the function of poetry. Classical critics expected poetry to instruct as well as please and even emphasized its instructive function. Romanticism aimed at mere artistic pleasure through the expression of an intensely emotional experience. The poet is a poet mainly because of his power of *feeling* intensely. Wordsworth's poet not only *feels* strongly, but also *thinks* deeply. To Wordsworth, "Poetry is the breath and finer spirit of all knowledge."[4] Poetry sharpens our power of not only feeling, but also of thinking. Thus Wordsworth believes in the didactic function of poetry as well as the aesthetic one. This awareness of the didactic function brings some classical element in Wordsworth's poetics.

Wordsworth's poetry sometimes became defective, according to some critics, because of his too much didactic motive. J.C. Smith, for example, observes, "Two defects remain in which theory and temperament seem to conspire. The first is a tendency to didacticism. We resent poetry which, in Keats's phrase, 'has a design upon us.' Wordsworth once told Lady Beaumont that he wished to be regarded as a teacher or as nothing. A natural wish in a dedicated spirit, but its insistence sometimes made him forget Dryden's golden maxim, a maxim which he accepted in theory [classical influence—was Dryden not classical?] that Poesy only instructs as it delights. This tendency grew on him in and after *The Excursion.* His poetic fire was dying down, but he still had much of value to say, and used his proved accomplishment of verse to say it in."[5] Thus Wordsworth's critical belief and poetic practice show his strong awareness of the didactic function of poetry—a characteristic of classicism.

After commenting on the democratic and classical elements in Wordsworth's *Preface to Lyrical Ballads*, I want to examine the truth in Wordsworth's application of his theory of poetic diction to Gray's (Gray said, 'The language of the age is never the language of poetry'[6]) Sonnet on the Death of Richard West, to reconsider his views on poetic diction.

> In vain to me the smiling mornings shine,
> And reddening Phoebus lifts his golden fire
> The birds in vain their amorous descant join,
> Or cheerful fields resume their green attire.
> These ears, alas for other notes repine;
> *A different object do these eyes require;*
> *My lonely anguish melts no heart but mine;*
> *And in my breast the imperfect joys expire;*
> Yet morning smiles the busy race to cheer,
> And new-born pleasure brings to happier men;
> The fields to all their wonted tribute bear;
> To warm their little loves the birds complain.
> *I fruitless mourn to him that cannot hear,*

And weep the more because I weep in vain.

After quoting this sonnet Wordsworth observes in his *Preface to Lyrical Ballads*: "It will easily be perceived, that the only part of this Sonnet which is of any value is the lines printed in Italics; it is equally obvious, that, except in the rhyme, and in the use of the single word 'fruitless' for fruitlessly, which is so far a defect, the language of these lines does in no respect differ from that of prose."

It is difficult to believe that the part of the Sonnet not printed in italics has no value. Nor is it possible to accept that the language of the lines printed in italics does not differ from that of prose. In this Sonnet the poet expresses his awareness of the intensity of vanity of the beauty and the pleasant things around him, and the vanity of his weeping for Richard West. He has suggested the intensity of his feeling by means of contrast and devices such as repetition, inversion and personification. All the lines of the Sonnet have contributed to the final effect—not only the lines printed in italics. Therefore it is difficult to understand why Wordsworth says only the lines printed in italics are of any value.

Nor does it seem completely true that the language of the lines printed in italics does not differ from that of prose. Any one can note the following deviations from the language of prose: The lines in italics are no. 6 to 8 and the last two (13 and 14). Line no. 6 contains inversion—The order of words in prose would be "these eyes do require a different object." In line no. 7 the word "melts" is metaphorically used, though to "melt heart" may be idiomatically used in prose. Besides in view of the fact that the grammatical subject of the verb "melt" is "anguish," one may have a slight perception of personification in that line (no. 7). In line no. 8 "joys" are personified and the word "expire" is used metaphorically. The deviation in line no. 13 is acknowledged by Wordsworth himself. Perhaps only in line no. 14 there is no deviation from prose. But even in it one may slightly perceive the use of the device of repetition.

Thus everybody may not share Wordsworth's opinion about the language of Gray's Sonnet. He could have illustrated his point better by taking examples from Blake's short poems. But perhaps

Blake was not an acknowledged poet then. Before quoting Gray's Sonnet Wordsworth has said (in his *Preface to Lyrical Ballads*), "And it would be a most easy task to prove to him, [the reader] that not only the language of a large portion of every good poem, even of the most elevated character, must necessarily, except with reference to the metre, in no respect differ from that of good prose, but likewise that some of the most interesting parts of the best poems will be found to be strictly the language of prose when prose is well written. The truth of this assertion might be demonstrated by innumerable passages from almost all the poetical writings, even of Milton himself." The statements in this quotation do not seem true. Wordsworth has stated the possibility of demonstrating the truth, but he has tried to do it only with reference to Gray's Sonnet. Even there he seems to fail.

Wordsworth seems to have suggested in the passage quoted above that the poetry not written in the language of prose is not good. This may not seem true to most students and critics of poetry. One should try to find out what passages from Milton Wordsworth was likely to have in his mind when he significantly added "even of Milton himself." On the contrary, Wordsworth himself seems to have adopted Milton's style in some parts of his poems. Look at, for example, the following extract from "Lines Written a Few Miles above Tintern Abbey":

> These beauteous forms,
> Through a long absence, have not been to me
> As is a landscape to a blind man's eye:
> But oft, in lonely rooms, and 'mid the din
> Of towns and cities, I have owed to them,
> In hours of weariness, sensations sweet,
> Felt in the blood, and felt along the heart;
> And passing even into my purer mind,
> With tranquil restoration—feelings too
> Of unremembered pleasure: such, perhaps,
> As have no slight or trivial influence
> On that best portion of a good man's life,
> His little, nameless, unremembered, acts
> Of kindness and of love. Nor less, I trust,

> To them I may have owed another gift,
> Of aspect more sublime; that blessed mood,
> In which the burthen of the mystery,
> In which the heavy and the weary weight
> Of all this unintelligible world,
> Is lightened—that serene and blessed mood,
> In which the affections gently lead us on,—
> Until, the breath of this corporeal frame
> And even the motion of our human blood
> Almost suspended, we are laid asleep
> In body, and become a living soul:
> While with an eye made quiet by the power
> Of harmony, and the deep power of joy,
> We see into the life of things."

In this extract, besides the use of blank verse, Milton's influence seems apparent in the syntactic features of the language. A look at the punctuation will show that this passage of more than a score of lines has only two sentences. Do we have, except in the language of law and Banabhatta's Sanskrit *Kadambari,* such long sentences in good prose? Nor is the passage without any rhetorical devices. One can see examples of litotes, transferred epithet, personification, inversion, alliteration, archaic diction and circumlocution.

Thus it is possible to conclude that there are democratic and classical elements in the *Preface to Lyrical Ballads*, and there can be serious doubts about Wordsworth's comments on Gray's language (in his Sonnet) in the *Preface to Lyrical Ballads* as evidence to prove his views on the language of poetry. To remove the contradiction in labelling Wordsworth both classical and romantic, it may be said that every poet displays qualities of classicism and romanticism in more or less degree. We call him romantic when romantic qualities dominate and classical when classical. Thus the distinction between classicism and romanticism is relative or a matter of degree. Wordsworth seems also realistic in comparison with other romantic poets. One can see irony and paradox in the similarity between Wordsworth and T.S. Eliot—both were innovative, yet Wordsworth is known as romantic and Eliot antiromantic and classical. Innovation stamped Wordsworth romantic, but Eliot classical.

NOTES

1. "A poet is a nightingale, who sits in darkness and sings to cheer its own solitude with sweet sounds." P.B. Shelley, "A Defence of Poetry."
2. P.B. Shelley, the last sentence of "A Defence of Poetry."
3. "The end of poetry is to produce excitement in co-existence with an overbalance of pleasure; but, by the supposition, excitement is an unusual and irregular state of the mind; ideas and feelings do not, in that state, succeed each other in accustomed order. If the words, however, by which this excitement is produced be in themselves powerful, or the images and feelings have an undue proportion of pain connected with them, there is some danger that the excitement may be carried beyond its proper bounds. Now the co-presence of something regular, something to which the mind has been accustomed in various moods and in a less excited state cannot but have great efficacy in tempering and restraining the passion by an intertexture of ordinary feeling and of feeling not strictly and necessarily connected with the passion." William Wordsworth, *Preface to Lyrical Ballads*.
4. William Wordsworth, *Preface to Lyrical Ballads*.
5. J.C. Smith, *A Study of Wordsworth* (Oliver and Boyd, 1946), Chapter V, p. 64. Wordsworth seems classical like Pope in his choice of verse for contents fit to be expressed in prose. Classical English poetry seemed prosaic to many critics, and so did much of Wordsworth's verse.
6. *Correspondence*, ed. Toynbee and Whibley (1935), p. 192.

Is There a Nightingale in Keats's "Ode to a Nightingale"?

S. KANNAMMAL

In reading of Keats's "Ode to a Nightingale" I gain the perception that the text speaks not of the Nightingale but of the indeterminacies of experiences and contexts. To me it appears, that this impossibility to assert any certainties and Nagarjuna's (the second century Mahayana Buddist teacher) 'doctrine of void' has much in common. This may seem a wild claim and a far-fetched one and I will not be taken as a serious scholar. But I seek to defend myself against such a charge.

As a first attempt at this defence I would like to speak about the space in which I am placed that confronts and excites a provocative site for criticism in reading the text of Keats. The Indian soci-historical-literary-cultural context that conditions my reading responses to Keats's text is so different from the cultural space of Keats in which he has produced his writings. Therefore it is very clear that I cannot think like Keats or have a feel of his sensibilities, which are a product of his immediate socio-cultural support system. It is also difficult and frustrating to adjust my critical thinking to the already expounded authoritative Euro-centric critical constructions on Keats. This is so because the critical authority to whom I have to adjust my thinking happens to be spaced in a different cultural context. If at all this is attempted, it debilitates the critical potentialities of a diverse and multifaceted critical space like that of the Indian context. This paper is an attempt in this direction of setting a mark, however small, for the Indian response, on the map of critical inquiry in the postcolonial and post-structuralist context. The Reader Theories and the post-structuralist literary practice offers enough scope for this task.

The present study of Keats's "Ode" and Nagarjuna's 'doctrine of void' is limited only to the indeterminacies of concept and contexts. As the Indian response, in an intertextual reading, reads into the text of "Ode to a Nightingale," it seems to me that the text more than speaking of the Nightingale points to the impossibility of asserting a determinate reality for any experience—pain or pleasure. All realities are alleged realities that turn out to be a falsity. This very condition throws up a space of void. A solution is constantly deferred as nothing is determinate. This knowledge of void of Maya is difficult to apprehend or accept. The Indian philosophical tradition is steeped in such complexities. The knowledge of voidness does not lead to nihilism or meaninglessness but provides a pragmatic and practical strategy to confront the issues like pain/pleasure and loss/gain. For an Indian reader like me conditioned in such a cultural context, indeterminacy means only this. Such a perception as it reads into Keats's Ode challenges the certainty of the notions of pleasure and pain and revises the assumption of the privileged position of the Nightingale in the text.

The title by referring to the Nightingale raises the expectations of the reader to find the text speaking of the Nightingale. But the text with its textual strategy of the opening remarks on the pain of the speaker belies this expectation: "*My* heart aches, and a drowsy numbness pains/*My* sense, as though of hemlock *I* had drunk." Therefore the text is a text of the other. The speaker seems to be suffering from some pain. But the slide in the text to the experience of happiness revises this opinion: "But being too happy in thine happiness." Does the text speak of a different experience or the same experience being labelled differently? The pain felt earlier might have caused the happiness or the happiness was the source of the pain. The bird could be the source of pain. The text seems to point to the bird's happiness and not the bird being the source of the speaker's happiness. If the bird could be happy it could also be unhappy.

The text suddenly shifts from talking about the bird to that of the desire of the speaker for a "draught of vintage." There is a further slide from this desire to the description of the "Dance, and Provencal song, and sunburnt mirth" of the people of the South.

It means that by and large people are happy in this world. But the speaker expresses the wish: "That I might drink, and leave the world unseen/ And with thee fade away into the forest dim." The wish is then to go from the context of the "sunburnt mirth" to that of the "forest dim."

Though the text speaks of the desire to "leave the world unseen," the elaborate details of the world and its sorrows point towards the speaker's obsession with the world. The speaker wants to forget as the text says: "to think is to be full of sorrow/ And leaden eyed despair." But the speaker does the opposite by thinking on it and listing a number of experiences of the world. This may mean that the narrator loves to indulge in the painful experiences. But why then he wants to flee from here? The speaker's attempt to expound in great detail such painful experiences and marginalize the bird by dubbing it as ignorant ("What thou has not known") shows the love of the speaker for the people who suffer the pain. The desire to leave the world unseen in this context would mean the speaker's love for the people who suffer and not the love for the bird. Yet the text speaks of the wish to fly to the bird: "Away! away! for I will fly to thee." The repetition of the word 'away' signals the desire of the speaker to be away from something than the desire to fly towards another thing. The speaker seems to have landed with the bird perhaps too suddenly: "Though the dull brain perplexes and retards/ Already with thee." Maybe the speaker is not all that happy to end the flight too soon. Perhaps he loves the flight for its own sake.

The speaker's desire to fly to the bird seemed to have been achieved but curiously enough the text indulges in describing the new space in great detail than the experience of being with the bird. The bird seems to have been marginalized in this different space and its experiences. But the narrator experiences difficulty in the darkness of the new space: "I cannot see what flowers are at my feet/ Nor what incense hangs upon the boughs." The speaker seems to find fault with this situation and he gets along fulfilling the task of knowing the colour and the smell: "But in embalmed darkness guess each sweet." Though the physical senses are absent, through an intellectual process, the experience is completed. The textual strategy of the elaborateness of such description points to the fact that the speaker never makes any serious attempt to locate the bird. On the other hand, the experiences of guessing each 'sweet' and 'murmurous haunt of flies' is enjoyed.

There is a sudden shift in the text as it speaks of the wish of the speaker to die. It is curious because while the worldly space "Where Beauty cannot keep her lustrous eyes" has inspired the flight to live with the bird, the "already with thee" condition had brought the wish to die. So this raises the question—which experience the Nightingale typifies? Does the text pinpoint, in specific terms, the experience or the context for which the Nightingale stands? Perhaps not.

The text seems to be silent about the bird. The speaker never seems to have located the bird. He could only listen; "Darkling I listen." If the bird is in darkness, why does it then sing "of summer in full-throated ease"? Does the song speak of the bird's desire to be in the sunshine? Maybe. The prediction of the speaker is that the ecstatic song would become a high requiem and sod. Is it the bird's own sad experiences that make the song sad or does the speaker impose his own state of mind on the emotional quality of the song? The Tamil poet Bharathi while looking at the black crow does not see the colour of the bird but he sees there his Lord. The specificity of the bird disappears. Here in this context the speaker's obsession with his notions and experiences seems to be enumerated than any attempt on the part of the text to speak of the specific bird, Nightingale. The text nowhere except in the title mentions the name Nightingale. Therefore the Nightingale bird referred to in the title and the bird referred to by the text need not necessarily be the same. Further the text speaking of the immortal voice heard by a variety of people—the king, the Clown and Ruth—privileges the voice over the bird. The contexts and the experiences of the listeners to the voice are varied and defy fixedness. Therefore there is no Nightingale in this text. It is impossible to find a simple referent to the term. What the term succeeds in referring to consists of traces of experiences and these traces are traces of traces.

Further the question that the text poses, "Was it a vision, or a waking dream?" challenges the alleged reality of the Nightingale. The speaker does not know whether he/she is awake or asleep but he/she has the knowledge that the state defies any certainty. The contexts of experiences are constituted with an infinite play of differences that defy a static definition of both, the experiences as well as the contexts. The text perhaps calls the language as the 'deceiving elf' that defies a simple reference in determinate terms about any experience. The text fails to fix the categories of pain/pleasure, sleeping/waking, darkness/light, loss/gain.

This indeterminacy caused by the text, in my point of view, instead of leading to nihilism rather throws light upon the need to confront the consequences of such indeterminacy. The text does not speak of the reality but the absence of it which is the case with life. The need for the knowledge about this voidness in order to confront the voidness itself is what the text speaks about. It gives a knowledge to engage the issues of life rather than a theory of reality.

Shelley as a Visionary and a Rebel with a Cause: A Retrospect

ZEENAT B. MERCHANT

Kelvin Everest in his observations on the bicentenary essays on Shelley remarks: "Today, thanks, partly to recent editorial efforts by scholars in Britain and America and partly to the changed and more liberal atmosphere that now generally prevails in British literary culture and academic life, Shelley's stature is again high. Today, Shelley is understood as the greatest poet of the political left."[1]

The modern era is a witness to a number of critics, who have addressed themselves to the revival and resurgence of Shelley in the contemporary literary scenario. They have re-evaluated his poetry and prose in terms of critical theories of Feminism, Deconstruction, Stylistics and of futuristic, comparative and inter-textual analyses. The concentration of my paper is on the reassessment of P.B. Shelley as a radical thinker, a mythopoeic poet, an incomparable master of lyric, a defender of poetry and imagination in an age dominated by Mammon worship and above all, Shelley as a visionary and a rebel with a cause.

Kenneth Cameron reveals that Shelley was "the product of a school of thought—its most penetrating creative thinker in fact—stretching from Jefferson to Cobbett, from Diderot to Godwin; a school arising out of the American and French Revolution and the English reform movement."[2] Shelley's poetry reveals his pursuit of millennium, which postulates that without passing through a painful process of destruction, the prospects for the advent of the golden age are remote. This theory has been exemplified in the course of my study on Shelley.

> it was hunger now, but thirst. Each well
> was choked with rotten corpses, and became
> A cauldron of green mist made visible
> At sunrise.
>
> Naked they were from torture, without shame
> spotted with nameless scars and lubrid blains
> Childhood, and age writhing in
> savage pains.

The above lines written by Shelley in the *The Revolt of Islam* (1818) suggest, that the period of thirty years (1792-1822), in which the life of Shelley was cast, was a time of turmoil. Plague, Famine and Slaughter were the effects of the War. The French Revolution also had far-reaching consequences. This was also the time of innovation, repression and fierce conflicts between governors and subjects. The first quarter of the eighteenth century, with which Shelley's literary career almost coincided, it was perhaps the gloomiest of all. Under Lord Eldon, civil and religious liberty was for the time trampled underfoot, while the social condition of the working classes grew more desperate every year.

With the coming of the Industrial Revolution, Science reached great heights. Shelley in *The Defence of Poetry* (1821) says that with the cultivation of the sciences, "man having enslaved the elements, remains himself, a slave." He further proclaims that "the principle of Self, of which money is the visible incarnation—are God and Mammon of the world." Science had mechanized life to such an extent that Man had forgotten to exist as an individual and as a human being. People disillusioned by the Church had moved away from spiritualism and mortality. Even in literature, as in politics, it was an age of conflict and revolution. The monotonous tyranny of the correct school of poetry, of which Pope may stand as the representative was giving way to a simpler and more natural style, of which Cowper and Burns were the forerunners and Wordsworth, the first apostle. Keir Hardie once said: "If anything is to be accomplished in this world, it must be done by visionaries, by men and women who can see the future and make the future because they can see it." The statement also seems to be the clarion call of the Romantic Movement, which started around the year 1770. The movement affected the arts and culture in general, but in essence, it was a reaction against the eighteenth century civilization and concentrated on insight, imagination and the individual. They saw things to which the ordinary intelligence is blind. As Blake says in "Auguries of Innocence":

> To see the world in a grain of sand,
> And heaven in a wild flower;
> Hold infinity in the palm of your hand,
> And eternity in an hour.

Every poet has to work with the senses, but for the Romantic, it was the instrument which set their visionary powers in action. It affected them at times in such a way that they seemed to be carried beyond it, into a transcendental order of things. This is obviously true for Wordsworth, Keats, Blake, Coleridge and Shelley, who brought back to poetry a keenness of eye and of ear. My study shall centre around Percy Bysshe Shelley, whose name became synonymous with the word 'revolution.'

A Romantic poet of the second generation, Shelley was born at Field Place, Harsham Sussex on August 4th, 1792. He was an apostle of dreams and considered it part of his poetic mission, to become inspirer and guide of men. To understand Shelley fully, we need to concentrate on his philosophical, religious, moral, social and political views, and his views on literature and art.

Shelley was an idealist. He became discontented with the cold and colourless tenets of materialism and by 1815 had adopted the immaterial philosophy of Berkeley, who asserted that one needs to penetrate the cloak of appearances and grasp the reality underlying all forms. This idea recurs in the following lines of *Prometheus Unbound* (1820):

> Man, one harmonious soul of many a soul,
> Whose nature is its own divine control

establishing the theory that behind the changing many there is a constant one, behind the delusive appearance of the material is the eternal reality of the Ideal.

Through Shelley's religious beliefs, we come to know that he believed in the coexistence of Good and Evil and its inevitability typified by Laon and Cythna, by the serpent and the eagle, the king and his subjects, the church and its people. But at the same time, Shelley also believed in the free will of human beings and the power of regenerated imagination to transform the world.

Shelley called himself an atheist. In "Queen Mab" (1813) for instance, when he speaks of God, he evidently uses the name in a theological sense where God seems to signify the soul of the universe, in which Shelley certainly believed. He adopted the name 'atheist' in a spirit of chivalrous defiance against the then-existing Christian beliefs. In the contemporary times too, with science and religion at crossroads, Atheism has become an arena treaded on by many individuals.

Shelley's attitude of Christianity resembled that of Blake. He condemned thc dogmas of Christian faith and felt it a duty to utter opinions plainly on the subject. He felt that the spirit of established Christianity was wholly out of harmony, with that of its founder Jesus Christ. He said that if a second Jesus Christ should arise in these days, his fate would be lengthened imprisonment and infamous punishment. In *Prometheus Unbound*, he writes:

> A woeful sight a youth
> With patient looks nailed to a crucifix.

A great gulf continued to separate him from the contemporary expressions of Christianity. He did not believe in the original sin. His mission was to prepare actively for the destined hour and a human spirit made ready for it by courageous resistance to evil. Shelley did not think of repentance as another of the Christian virtues; in fact he condemns it in his poem "The Revolt of Islam," saying that it is useless brooding over the past which retards the omnipotence of man's will in the future. He claimed for himself and for others, absolute freedom of opinion in religious matters. Shelley believed that if we set aside the tyranny of custom and allow scope for the intuitive excellence of our true nature for original goodness and not original sin, it would be the rejuvenation of mankind.

Art Young, in a chapter entitled "Shelley and Gandhi," gives us a new dimension to criticism on Shelley, for he views the poet as a pioneer of non-violence, forbearance and passive resistance in early nineteenth century England. He proclaims that "Shelley's interpretation of history is remarkably similar to Gandhi's." In the words of Dverkson, "Shelley interprets history as a persistent struggle between dictatorship and liberty in which the general tendency is towards liberty."

"Queen Mab" is an expression of Shelley's early political and social ideas. It reflects the social evils inflicted on common people by the conspiracy of kings and priests. Shelley was conscious of the harm the social, political and religious institutions could do to the ignorant masses. In "Queen Mab" Shelley assumes that reason must triumph and that it will bring wealth and liberty, abolish hunger and poverty, make the earth supply human needs and assuage the sting of suffering.

In his "Address to the Irish People" (1812) Shelley condemns war as a criminal and foolish practice. He deprecated cruelty and violence of all kinds. He was too large-hearted to be able to restrict his benevolence to mankind alone; he thus advocated vegetarianism in his "Vindication of Natural Diet" (1813).

Shelley looked at Nature with a pantheistic view. Man himself is a part of nature and turns to her for comfort and guidance. Shelley's Skylark, his cloud, his West Wind are untroubled by the misery of man. Man can, according to Shelley, regain composure from the hardships of civilizations, in the company of nature. Love is a term equivalent to liberty and nature. It is the great power through which the world may be regenerated. In *Prometheus Unbound*, he writes:

Wisdom, Justice, Love, Peace
When they struggle to increase
Are to us soft winds be
To shepherd boys the prophecy
Which begins and ends in thee.

The mythopoeic imagination can be seen at work, as Shelley uses the tragedy of Aeschylus as a model, with the story of how Prometheus was bound to a rock by Jupiter. He modifies the legend to glorify the spirit that man might have if he would take love as his guiding law and refuse to tolerate any form of tyranny. The theme of the poem revolves around the moral salvation of man.

We also see a Social Reformer in Shelley, who believed firmly in the emancipation of women. He painted in glowing colours the happiness that might result, if women could break the bonds of restraint imposed on them by ignorance and custom and stand forth as the free and equal companions of men. In "The Revolt of Islam," this vision is presented in its fullest form as Cythnia is shown as the fearless liberator. The poem is also a revelation of the poet's firm conviction that man cannot be free 'if woman be a slave' nor can be defeat the oppressor if she is condemned to hear scorn. "The Revolt of Islam" unfolds a universal phenomenon of conflict between the good and the evil. The poem reaffirms the value of liberty and justice and illustrates the growth and progress of individual mind aspiring after excellence and devoted to the love of mankind.

Shelley's criticism of the Literature and Art during his time can be seen in "The Defence of Poetry." Shelley says that the scope of art is to portray the impression made on man, in his contact with nature and society. Poetry being the most direct way of doing this, Shelley attempts to find a natural and social explanation that is in accord with the science of his day. He believed that beauty constitutes the essence of art as truth constitutes the essence of reasoning and that pleasure, virtue and love are obviously all as much a part of art, as they are of human communication.

Concerning idealism in poetry, Shelley was influenced by Plato. In all ethical and political questions of the day, he was a follower of Godwin. Kant in large way influenced his imagination and art, so did Dante's elevated style of writing.

In Shelley's lyrics one finds intensity of expression, beauty and the perfect harmony between metre and the subject matter. Shelley's lyricism is, in the words of Wordsworth, 'a spontaneous overflow of emotions'; it is inspired and natural. Shelley's best lyrics are his nature poems like "To a Skylark" (1820) and "The Cloud" (1820). Although "Ode to the West Wind" (1820) appears to be a nature poem, it does not contain merely a description of a storm; it is a symbolic poem. Shelley regards the West Wind as a symbol of energy and freedom. He looks upon the dead leaves as a symbol of the old social and political order and regards the new leaves as a symbol of the new reign or age of light, love and happiness.

When it comes to T.S. Eliot's "Tradition and the Individual Talent" (1919) or Roland Barthes's "Death of the Author" (1968) one would be wary of the biographical snare, but in Shelley's poems, one tends to find a confessional note. For example, the fourth part of "Ode to the West Wind" reveals a note of personal despair as he says:

> Oh, lift me as a wave, a leaf, a cloud!
> I fall upon the thorns of life! I bleed!

Shelley appeals to the West Wind for help because he feels that he is bound up in chains of social and political conventions and because he lacks both energy and freedom. As the thorns pierce Shelley's heart, the raptures make him utter:

> Our sweetest songs are those that tell of saddest thought

One of the major reasons for Shelley's suffering is that he never accepted things as he found them. Even when in school, he was called 'mad Shelley' due to his rebellious nature. When he went to Oxford his pamphlet "The Necessity of Atheism" (1811) brought a conflict with the officials. Shelley lived among ideas which were at war with many accepted standards of his time, but the fact remains that the prophetic visions that Shelley had, have today, transformed into reality. One of the instances of this can be found in "A Philosophical View of Reform" (1820) in which he wrote:

> We would abolish the national debt
> We would disband the standing army.

He further proclaimed that we would with every possible regard to the existing interests of the holders abolish tithes and make all religions, all forms of opinion respecting the origin and government of the universe equal in the eye of the law and also that we would make justice cheap, certain and speedy and extend the institution of juries to every possible occasion of jurisprudence.

Today we have done away with war and the ideal of Democracy has been achieved where the citizens of a Democratic nation enjoy the Fundamental Rights given to them by the constitution, which states that the nation is a socialist secular and a Democratic Republic under which all religions are to be respected and men and women enjoy equal status.

Shelley's ability to transcend the materialistic world and delve into the spiritual is resorted to by the poets and writers in the modern era. The confessional note found in certain poems of Shelley, where the individual is the central motif, is what Modern Poetry today concentrates on.

Moreover, the prerequisites for writing poetry mentioned in "The Defence of Poetry" have also been inculcated by modern poets which is evident in their works. Apart from this, the views on the emancipation of women, put forward by Shelley are the views exhorted by many Feminists of the contemporary times. Hence Shelley is not as Matthew Arnold called him, "A beautiful and ineffectual angel, beating his luminous wings in vain." It was the world which was not ready to receive the angel whose luminous wings act as a guiding light and whose raptures still exhort us

> To suffer woes which Hope thinks infinite
> To forgive wrongs darker than death or night;
> To defy power, which seems omnipotent
> To love and bear, to Hope creates;
> From its own wreck the thing it contemplates;
> Neither to change, nor falter, nor repent;
> . . . to be
> Good great and joyous, beautiful and free
> This is alone Life, Empire and Victory.
>
> (*Prometheus Unbound*, Act IV)

NOTES

1. Kelvin Everest, ed., *Percy Bysshe Shelley: Bicentenary Essays* (1992).

2. K.N. Cameron. *The Young Shelley: Genesis of a Radical* (London: Victor Gollancz, 1951).
3. S. Aiyar, *Shelley: Poetry and Prose* (Bombay: Karnatak Publishing House, 1945).
4. E.H. Blakeney, ed., *Selections from Shelley* (London: Macmillan, 1926).
5. D.J. Enright and E.D. Chickera, ed., *English Critical Texts, 16th Century to 20th Century* (London: Oxford University Press, 1962).
6. T. Hutchinson, ed., *The Complete Poetical Works of Percy Bysshe Shelley* (London: Oxford University press, 1927).
7. A.M.D. Hughes, *Shelley: Poetry and Prose* (London: Oxford University Press, 1952).

Drama in the Romantic Age: A Re-Assessment

M.N. CHATTERJEE

As in life, so in literature, it is one thing to form a theory; it is quite a different and difficult thing to execute that theory in practice; and it is for the next generation to judge how far the man or the age conformed to the theory. In our study of English romantic literature, specially drama, the most baffling point is this relation between theory and practice. The age has been denounced unanimously by the critics for its deficiency in dramatic writing; but at the same time the age is a landmark in the history of English dramatic criticism. The most curious point to note is that all the major romantic poets, who assayed to write drama, were aware of this infertility of the age and they believed that the absence of serious drama originated from some specific failure of understanding or some particular material contingency. To them, the vitality of the drama was inseparable from the health of body politic. Shelley's argument in *Defence of Poetry* (published in 1840), "And it is indisputable that the highest perfection of human society has ever corresponded with the highest dramatic excellence; and that the corruption or the extinction of the drama in a nation where it has once flourished, is a mark of a corruption of manners and an extinction of the energies which sustain the soul of social life,"[1] comes from the realisation that the periods of classic, Spanish, Elizabethan and French drama coincided with the periods of particular national energy. Hazlitt felt that there has occurred in the spirit of the age some great disillusion—the nervous, paradoxical temper of the time could produce lyric poetry, but it lacked the confidence required for drama. In spite of this lack, there was, at the heart of the age, an impulse towards drama and, as George Steiner suggests, "at the origins of the romantic movement lies an explicit attempt to revitalize the major forms of tragedy."[2] In fact, romanticism began as a critique of the failure of the eighteenth century to carry on the great traditions of the Elizabethan theatre. In a letter to Byron, Coleridge spoke of "the tragic Dwarfs, which exhausted Nature seem to have been under the necessity of producing since Shakespeare."[3] Sir Walter Scott boldly declared "the age has no reason to apprehend any decay of dramatic talent"[4]; but a careful study of the contemporary writing reveals the fact that in spite of their sincerest attempt to "revitalize" drama, they had failed to grasp those genuine essentials on which "dramatic talent" must be based, or without which this talent cannot hope to succeed.

The reason behind this decline, both Shelley and Hazlitt suggest, is "the soul of social life" or the spirit of the age, and this tendency of conferring responsibility on the contemporary society, can be observed in the later critics. From their observations we can divide these reasons into two groups—the internal and the external. Drama, which is the most social of all literary forms, is certainly guided by some social factors and in our consideration of degeneration in dramatic writing we must take into account these external factors as well as the inherent demerits of the dramatists themselves. Allardyce Nicoll has studied this problem, splitting it into a series of questions and in a literary-historian fashion he holds the view that the failure of the famous romantic poets as dramatists was a part of the general failure of the age as a whole.[5] He is not ready to level the age as "lyric" as distinguished from the "dramatic" spirit of the Elizabethan England, but he thinks that the lyrical triumphs of the romantics made them weak in playwriting. Truly, lyric mood may exist along with the dramatic one, as Shakespeare and Webster testify, but, according to Nicoll, "the dramatic mood ultimately depends on a sense of humour."[6] Nicoll's explanation of this "sense of humour" is similar to Keats's famous theory of Negative Capability and it is not correct to equate the sense of humour with Negative Capability, because the sense of humour originates from insight and the sympathy with the object; it is the power to look at a thing in its true proportion; while Negative Capability is something more than this—an ability to forget one's own identity and merge it into others. The Jacobean dramatists have written good dramas despite their lack of this "sense"; and, again, one may ask why Charles Lamb, in spite of his good sense of humour, has failed to pen any dramatic work of high merit. However, Nicoll is right to assert that the predominance of the lyric mood—the "intruding I"—has opposed the romantics to write any great drama, because both tragedy and comedy depend upon the author's ability to forget his own petty loves and woes and to transform these to the universal. This the poets, as they were always feeling subjectively, failed to do.

This "intruding I" or obsession with the self has been inherited by the Romantics, suggests George Steiner in *The Death of Tragedy*, from Rousseau. The famous opening statement of Rousseau's *Confessions*, "I want to show to my fellowmen a man in all the truth of nature and that man will be I. I alone. I feel my own heart, and know men. I am not made up like any that I have seen; I venture to believe that I am unlike any that exist"[7] strikes the central chord in romantic literature. While the classical temper censured a work of art if the author revealed in it his own person or private sensibility, the romantics sought in art the rapture of self-consciousness; they placed the ego at the centre of the intelligible world. Being the natural voice of self-consciousness, the lyric is the dominant mode of romantic literature which disallows them to write great dramas. Doubtless, the creation of a dramatic character is related to the private genius of the dramatist, but whatever may be their relationship to the source of invention, the dramatic personages assume their own integral being and they lead their own life far beyond the mortality of the playwright. Thus, what we need in a drama is this intelligent blending of "private genius" and the character's own "integral being." In fact, the romantics went so far as to render the poem inseparable from the voice of the poet, and in the romantic imagination, expression invariably tended towards self-portrayal. Such a conception was radically inappropriate to drama and yet the romantics sought to bring the dramatic form within the scope of egotism.

It is true that all the major romantic poets were not blind to the contradiction between an egotistical theory of art and the nature of drama and in this respect Keats was an exception. He was an antiromantic in his ideal of drama founded on a rejection of what he called the "egotistical sublime." Keats asserted: "Men of genius are great as certain ethereal Chemicals operating on the Mass of neutral intellect—but they have not any individuality, any determined character." In October 1818, he described his conception of the true poet: "As to the poetical character itself . . . it is not itself—it is everything and nothing—It has no character—it enjoys light and shade; it lives in gusto, be it foul or fair, high or low, rich or poor, mean or elevated—It has so much delight in conceiving an Iago as an Imogen. . . . A poet is the most unpoetical of anything in existence; because he has no Identity." In the same month, Keats wrote to his brother: "I do live in this world alone, but in a thousand worlds. . . . According to my state of mind I am with Achilles shouting in the trenches, or with Theocritus in the Vales of Sicily. Or I throw my whole being into Troilus. . . . I melt into the air."[8] Keats's recognition of the manner in which the dramatic poet is annihilated within his work is superbly classical. It refutes the entire Rousseauist and romantic conception of the primacy of the self.

If the romantic movement inherited from Rousseau his obsession with the self, it inherited also his presumption of natural goodness and his belief in the social rather than metaphysical origin of evil and in the perfectibility of man. From the tragedies written by the romantics it appears that many of them held an optimistic attitude towards the human condition. Neither in classical nor in Elizabethan literature man enjoys less importance, but in the romantic revival a shifing of emphasis has occurred. In the Rousseauist mythology of conduct, a man could commit a crime either because his education had not taught him how to distinguish between good and evil, or because he had been corrupted by society. Thus, responsibility lay with his schooling or environment for evil cannot be native to the soul. As the individual is not wholly responsible, he cannot be wholly damned. In the hour of truth, the criminal will be possessed by remorse; and the crime will be undone, or the error made good. Such a view of the human condition in spite of its psychological and Christian background, is not suitable for tragic drama, and it is this sense of remorse which runs through the entire romantic drama, and prevents the authors from writing any great tragedy. Remorse in the sense of suffering or biting agony is, in fact, not contrary to the tragic spirit of a drama as Marlowe's *Doctor Faustus*, Milton's *Samson Agonistes*, Shakespeare's *Macbeth* and *King Lear*, and T.S. Eliot's *The Family Reunion* testify. Remorse is there in all these tragedies, but it comes at such a moment when the protagonist has nothing left to hold on to; and he has to succumb. Even in Attic tragedy like *Oedipus at Colonus* and *The Eumenides*, the protagonists are to some extent excused, but their tragic lot cannot be altered. So, this sense of time and that of balance is very important in applying this theme of remorse in a tragedy. But the mechanism of timely remorse of redemption through love, which some of the romantic writers like Shelley and Lamb have adopted is seriously opposed to the tragic spirit. In his preface to *The Cenci*, Shelley disfavours "revenge, retaliation and atonement" and he advocates "a resolution to convert the injurer from his dark passions by peace and love."[9] In *Prometheus Unbound*, Prometheus is sublimated through Asia, symbol of love and in the last act of this lyrical drama the whole world rejoices at the happy dawn. John Woodvil, the hero of Charles Lamb's tragedy, is also forgiven after his repentance:

> I wept a second flood
> More poignant than the first;
> But afterwards was greatly comforted.
> It seem'd, the guilt of blood was passing from me
> Even in the act and agony of tears,
> And all my sins forgiven[10]

and then, we may guess, he enjoys the sweet embrace of his beloved, Margaret. Thus, the theme of remorse in the sense of redemption spoils the tragedy.

But this is not so in other romantic poets. Coleridge's Ancient Mariner is forgiven, but neither is he sublimated nor is he able to come back to normality. His glittering eye and ghostly appearance are enough to express the sufferings he has undergone. When the murderous villain, who is responsible for the evils committed in Wordsworth's tragedy, *The Borderers*, is told at the close of the play:

Thy office, thy ambition, be henceforth
To feed remorse, to welcome every sting
Of penitential anguish, yea with tears[11]

we can easily feel the tragic lot into which he is thrown. Again, Coleridge has used this theme in his play *Remorse*, but with a slight variation. When Ordonio, the villain of the play declares

. . . remorse! remorse!
Where gott'st thou that fool's word?
Curse on remorse!
Can it give up the dead or recompact
A mangled body? mangled—dashed to atoms!
Not all the blessings of a host of angels
Can blow away a desolate widow's curse!
And though thou spill thy heart's blood for atonement,
It will not weigh against an orphan's tear![12]

he offers a strong resistance to this idea of penitence but it is he who at last cries for 'atonement' at the cost of his own life. So, in this sense, the play is a tragedy, at least for Ordonio. Ordonio's temporary defiance has been carried to the extreme by Manfred, the hero of Byron's drama. Manfred has determined in his mad pride, that his punishment must be commensurate with his mysterious crime, he will not give himself absolution. He says to the avenging Spirit:

I have not been thy dupe; nor am thy prey—
But was own destroyer, and will be
My own herenafter.[13]

There is in this final arrogance a grim justice, and it gives to the close of *Manfred* a touch of real tragedy. It is, therefore, evident that the theme of remorse is undoubtedly a sufficient condition for the absence of tragic spirit, but not a necessary one.

However, these inherent demerits of the romantics—the predominance of the lyric note and the belief in the perfectibility of man—have led them to write plays which are, as Steiner terms, "near tragedy," which means four acts of tragic violence and guilt are followed by a fifth act of redemption and innocence regained. "Near-tragedy" is precisely the compromise of an age which did not believe in the finality of evil. It represents the desire of the romantics to enjoy the privileges of grandeur and intense feeling associated with tragic drama without paying the full price. This price is the recognition of the fact that there are in the world mysteries of injustice, disasters in excess of guilt, and realities which do constant violence to our moral expectations. The redemptive theory allows the romantic hero to partake of the excitement of evil without bearing the real cost. This "near-tragedy" is another name for melodrama.

The preference for melodrama, which we observe so greatly among the romantic poets, leads us to some external, rather social factors. Drama, for its success, is completely dependent upon the cross-fertilization of Imagination and the society, specially of the audience. These spectators play a very important role in the dramatic writing of an age. Even Shakespeare, the mastermind of the dramatic art, was disgusted to present himself as a "motley" to the common people. But at the same time, he was the Genius who could create his audience rather than surrender to the public taste. The romantics, on the contrary, were in search of their audience, to re-create a living theatre. Nineteenth century was the classic age of low-cost mass printing—of Scott's and Jane Austen's novels, of the periodicals like *The Examiner*, *The Edinburgh Review*, *The Quarterly Review*, *Blackwood's Magazine*, *The London Magazine* and *The Westminster Review*. The French Revolution and the Napoleonic wars plunged ordinary men into the stream of history and throughout the eighteenth century the centre of social gravity shifted towards the middle classes. The revolution laid the ordinary people open to the pressure of experience and feeling which in earlier times, were the dangerous prerogatives of princes, statesmen and professional soldiers. So, man became more experienced and "historical" than his predecessors. The nineteenth-century spectator came to the theatre not to see a mirror reflecting nature manipulated by expert hands, but with a relaxed attitude, he wished to move from his daily problems and social anxieties into the repose of illusion. It is true that seeking entertainment from drama had also been there in the past, yet that was not the sole objective; but in the romantic period drama, became overwhelmingly a mere form of entertainment, and the middle class spectator was not prepared to take the risk of terror and revelation. These old themes for the most part did not receive applause, but were hissed out of the stage by the audience. In this connection, we may quote a few lines from Lamb's essay "On the Custom of Hissing at the Theatres" where he has taunted the contemporary audience in his own style: "Oh; Mr. Reflector, is it not a pity that the sweet human voice, which was given man to speak with, to sing with, to whisper tones of love in, to express compliance, to convey a favour, or to grant a suit,—that voice . . . that the musical expressive human voice should be converted into a rival of the noises of silly geese, and irrational, venomous snakes?" (15) Byron in his Preface to *Marino Faliero*, while giving his reasons for not writing for the stage, expressed "doubt of their [audience's] competency to judge, and his [the author's] certainty of his own impudence in electing them his judges"[15]; and in spite of the underlying vanity, his comment has a true significance to the intellect of the then middle-class bourgeois audience with its lack of literary background and its taste for pathos and happy endings. To cater to the popular demand of this new audience, to rival the drama of actual news, the playwrights of the period turned to melodrama; and feeling unconsciously the impossibility of devising dramatic material which should be in direct harmony with the spirit of the age, naturally went abroad for inspiration. Almost half of the plays written between 1800-1850 must have been suggested by French melodramatists Pixerecourt and Eugene Scribe. Though German drama exerted little direct influence, the interest in German literature was certainly there among the romantics as in 1799 the publishers took out innumerable editions of Kotzebue and Schiller and volumes of collected works of Goethe. While adapatation had ruled for generations on the London stage, facts force us to admit that never before were so many foreign dramas reworked for English audiences.

Along with this inclination towards foreign drama, the Elizabethan and Jacobean literature was also eagerly ransacked by the playwrights of the period. The publication of Lamb's *Specimens of English Dramatic Poets* in 1808 opened a treasure-house of rhetoric and tragic sentiment to the romantic pursuit of drama. This was the period when the long-buried works of the minor Elizabethans were unearthed, when the literary critics of the time made a new approach to Shakespeare, and when the theatre managers discovered that Shakespeare had in him the stuff of which excellent melodramas could be made. And therefore, all the Shakespearean tragedies appeared on the English stage as melodramas, and the characters of Lear and Othello were translated into terms of everyday existence. Not only the plays, but also the enigmatic life of Shakespeare himself initiated the romantic dramatists to write numerous plays.[16] Besides Shakespeare, Marlowe, Kyd, Webster and Ford also had a commanding influence on the romantic dramatists.

While this imitation and adaptation of foreign as well as Elizabethan and Jacobean dramas formed a considerable portion of the dramatic writings of this period, the dramatization of novels is also interesting and in this respect Scott was a mighty luminary who reflected its glory upon the so-called 'illegitimate' drama. In the Waverley novels, the playwrights found that there was for them a mint of money. The themes of Scott's novels are themselves inclined towards melodramatic atmosphere, and this atmosphere, when translated in terms of the stage, became still more pronounced. The romantic settings, the boldly drawn type characters, the clear differentiation of virtue and vice and the innumerable adventures—all these appealed to the age and led towards many an imitation.[17] This careless adaptation of narrative fiction led towards mere stringing together of the episodes and it was this episodical treatment which marred the workmanship of the early nineteenth century plays. The better works of France and Germany were neglected and only the lighter and the more spectacular pieces were seized upon. Finer dramatic technique was lost, characterisation was not sought for; incidents alone could make a direct and popular appeal.

The sub-standardisation of drama thus, occurred partly owing to the melodramatic tendency of the age, and partly due to the small pecuniary rewards given to the dramatists—which leads us to study the problem from a different angle. Truly, the drama of any period is not created entirely by the force of economic factors, but a study of theatrical history does convince us that such factors should largely be considered when we regard, not merely dramatic activity in general, but the particular writers attracted to this form of literary art. The fact that many of the best brains of the Elizabethan period were recruited to the service of the stage, must be attributed, partly at least, to the financial prospect and partly to the possibility of fame arising from theatrical authorship. This is the point where the romantic age was lacking and in fact in all the major and minor writers of this age we notice a confusion over the idea of getting money and fame out of dramatic writing. Lamb, being encouraged by Richard Wroughton's assurance of staging *Mr. H—* at Drury Lane Theatre, was very much hopeful about its prospect and wrote to Manning: "I shall get 200 pound from the theatre if *Mr. H* has a good run, and I hope 100 pound for the copyright. Nothing if it fails, and there never was a more ticklish thing. . . . If my little thing don't succeed I shall easily survive, having, as it were, compared to H.'s venture [Holcroft's *Vindictive Man*], but a sixteenth in the lottery."[18] Keats, after writing *Otho the Great*, depended to a great extent on Edumund Kean's characterisation of Ludolph for the betterment of his own fortune. He wrote to John Taylor: "Brown and I have together been engaged (this I should wish to remain secret) on a Tragedy which I have just finished and from which we hope to share moderate profits."[19] Wordsworth in his note to *The Borderers* spoke of his dispassionate attitude towards its staging and yet he remarked in brackets that "a successful play would in the then state of my finances have been a most welcome piece of good fortune."[20] In such a period, when the dramatist attempted to live by his pen he was forced to turn out many more dramas than his predecessors had done. The low remuneration offered to the playwrights, because of heavy amount of financial drain behind every production, encouraged a frenzied activity of quantity rather than quality. From 1818 to 1850 J.R. Planche produced over hundred and fifty plays, while Fitzballs' efforts seemed almost incalculable; and we cannot expect a work of high merit from these authors writing under hard necessity.

The explanation of these small sums given to dramatists depended upon a series of concomitant circumstances all tending to one result, the impoverishment of the manager. In spite of large theatres, the playhouses rarely could be made to pay. All devices were tried from raising the price to lowering it, but all went in vain. Costs were much higher. The then machinery of the stage demanded a group of property-men and apart from a capital expenditure for this machinery, there was a constant outlay for upkeep. Since the audience demanded spectacle, scenery and costume had to be kept rich. Most important was the star-system and the consequent rise in salaries. With the rise of the chief actors, the amount paid to minor players also increased. The age might not be important for its dramatic output, but it was the age of celebrated actors and actresses who ruled the stage for long time. Keats in his letter to Benjamin Bailey boldly declared: "One of my Ambitions is to make as great a revolution in modern dramatic writing as Kean has done in acting."[21] How far he was successful in his revolutionary attempt is questionable, but he had a clear fascination for Edumund Kean and it was more pronounced in his strong assertion that only Kean could portray the hot-blooded character of Ludolph. In her note to *The Cenci*, Mrs. Shelley has referred to a letter written by Shelley to a friend in London. Speaking of his desire to stage the drama at Covent Garden, Shelley remarked: "The principal character Beatrice is precisely fitted for Miss O'Neil, and it might even seem to have been written for her (God forbid that I should see her play it—it would tear my nerves to pieces)."[22] It was the actor who drew the public rather than the play, and the dramatist tried to write plays exactly tailored to the tastes and technical resources of a particular actor. On the one hand we have this infatuation for particular actors and actresses, and on the other we have the pungent criticism which these players had to bear. This 'star-system' was constantly blamed by contemporaries for the evil state of the drama; for it not only caused greater expense but also had a pernicious effect upon the work produced. Lamb in his essay on "The Artificial Comedy" as originally published in the *London Magazine*, made a circumstantial account, which he omitted later on, of the cold and stately manner in which John Kemble performed the part of Antonio, in Godwin's unfortunate play of that name: "John Kemble had made up his mind early that all the good tragedies which could be written, had been written; and he resented any new attempt. His shelves were full. The old standards were scope enough for his ambition."[23] Yet, Lamb had also a peculiar infatuation for Miss Kelly and he seemed to be encouraged when the principal part of Mr. H was given to Elliston.

We have, thus briefly reviewed the reasons—both internal and external—behind the lack of excellence of the romantic age in dramatic productions. In a society where the role of a theatre had been changed, the audience became hungry for something new with a general liking for melodramas, it was not possible for the romantics, with their own limitations to revive the lost glory of the Elizabethan stage. One point strikes us here and that is the absence of comedy. Shelley's *Oedipus Tyrannus*, or *Swellfoot the Tyrant* is almost the only instance worth mention, and this was a poor specimen of the writer's creative power. It is true that in this age we have no such good comedy as we had in earlier ages. In fact, the romantics did not attain to that degree of self-forgetfulness, an essential criterion for both tragedy and comedy, which would help them to transcend their own feelings into universality. They tried their best to revive the Shakespearean tradition and were very much conscious of the barrenness of the age. P.C. Ghosh has summed up the whole case in this manner: "The nineteenth century verse drama followed the traditional romantic manner of the Elizabethans, and sought to provide opportunities for the dominant actors for presenting strong emotions in a richly rhetorical style. Sometimes such plays were written without any reference to the taste of the audience or even any thought of production—only as projections of the dramatists' visions of an imaginary state. The dramatic form was used in such cases to make the projections possible."[24] And that is the traditional opinion about the romantic age, but if we free ourselves from the shackles of conventionality and cast an impartial glance at their endeavour, there are a few words to be said in their favour. While fully admitting the view that the romantic conception of mankind is contrary to the authentic tragic conception, we must not miss the new dimension which these poets tried to build. This is for the first time that the romantics tried to alleviate the grim consequences of a crime committed and to allow a ray of hope to pierce in. They might not believe in the scapegoat theory or the exemplary idea of punishment which the ancient tragic poets had exhibited, but with their strong belief in Catholicism they introduced the idea of forgiveness. Apparently it seems more acceptable, because everyday, apart from our original sin, we are committing offence for some reasons or other, and if there lies no hope of forgiveness we cannot survive. It is true that this idea has a cheap aspect as to the selling of Indulgence certificates or the service of the Confession Chamber to relieve the offence, but one has to maintain this precarious balance. We cannot expect permanent absolution for our repeated crimes and if we do not accept the lesson we have to bear the consequences. The villain in Wordsworth's *The Borderers*, or Coleridge's "Ancient Mariner" is left to reap the harvest of his crime and John Woodvil's outburst comes as a purgation of his evil deed. This is the new idea—an idea of adjustment and understanding—which the romantic dramatists had brought in. The idea may be opposed to serious tragedy, but we must hail its novelty. It opens before us a new chapter in the text of human tragedy, and a new interpretation of the problem of man and his tragic lot befitting the demand of the age.

But, in spite of this novelty in their ideas, all the great romantic poets failed miserably to translate their ideas into practice. They all soiled their hands with the dust of the theatre, but public appreciation for ever deluded them. When they were rejected, they accepted the fate with good grace; and were happy to consider their plays as closet-dramas.

The entry for January 12, 1821, in his diary, when Byron was at Ravenna, reads: "*Marino Faliero* was written for the closet." In a letter to Murray a few days later he referred to the tragedy as a "poem" and declared: "I have never written but for the solitary reader." In June the same year he was able to announce to Moore "another tragedy" [*Sardanapalus*] which was also "not for the stage."[25] Shelley's *Prometheus Unbound* and *Hellas* were dramas more of ideas than of action, and obviously they could not be staged. Though they are termed "lyrical dramas," yet they should be judged as "poems" expressing the poet's ambition and optimism. Shelley also took up the story of an Enchantress and a Pirate and he composed a dramatic fragment, which, according to Mrs. Shelley, "was undertaken for the amusement of the individuals who composed our intimate society."[26] Another closet drama written by Shelley was *Oedipus Tyrannus* or *Swellfoot the Tyrant*. About this play Mrs. Shelley wrote: "In the brief journal I kept in those days, I find recorded, in August 1820, Shelley 'begins *Swellfoot the Tyrant*, suggested by the pigs at the fair of San Giuliano.'. . . We were then at the Baths of San Giuliano. A friend came to visit us on the day when the fair was held in the square, beneath our windows: Shelley read to us his *Ode to Liberty*; and was riotously accompanied by the grunting of a quantity of pigs brought for sale to the fair. He compared it to the 'chorus of frogs' in the satiric drama of Aristophanes; and, it being an hour of merriment, and one ludicrous association suggesting another, he imagined a political satirical drama on the circumstances of the day, to which the pig would serve as chorus—and *Swellfoot* was begun."[27] Coleridge published *Zapolya* "as a Christmas tale" and translated *The Piccolomini* or *The First Part of Wallenstein* and *The Death of Wallenstein* from "the German of Schiller" and nowhere in his Prefaces did he express any desire for the stage. Moreover, in his note on the fly leaves of annotated copies (in Coleridge's handwriting) of these two dramas, Coleridge pointed out their "grievous faults."[28] Wordsworth in his short printed note attached to *The Borderers* in 1842 wrote:

> This Dramatic Piece as noticed in its title-page, was composed in 1795-96. It lay nearly from that time till within the last two or three months unregarded among my papers. . . . Having, however, impressions upon my mind which made me unwilling to destroy the Ms. I determined to undertake the responsibility of publishing it during my own life. . . . Accordingly it has been revised with some care; but as it was at first written, and is now published, without any view to its exhibition upon the stage, not the slightest alternation has been made in the conduct of the story, or the composition of the characters, above all, in respect to the two leading Persons of the Drama, I felt no inducement to make any change.[29]

From these pronouncements of the poets it is clear that they wrote dramas for readers, and not for spectators. We may say that there is nothing as absurd as closet drama, and yet the romantics wrote it. Immediately the question comes to our mind: if the romantics wanted to avoid the stage, why did they adopt the dramatic form? They might write in other literary forms. In answer we may say that both the epic and the tragic forms were all but extinct when the Romantic movement began and as we have already mentioned, the romantic poets thought it an honourable task to revitalize the Elizabethan dramatic standard in their own age. With this purpose in mind all of them tried to express their ideas and emotions in the form of drama as well as in poems; and undoubtedly they failed in their former attempt. Thus, there remains a gap between their ideas and practice.[30]

So far their dramatic theories are concerned, it is obvious to say that the major romantic poets are not theoreticians, particularly in the field of drama, in the sense that Aristotle, Horace and Longinus are regarded theorists. In fact, their writings on drama are so scanty, in an age chiefly known for its revolution in poetic language, that they are seldom noticed by the literary critics in the annals of dramatic criticism. However, the romantic poets' casual remarks on this subject can be gleaned from their prefaces, notes, and letters; and these are summed up under the broad-head of dramatic theory. It is curious to note that the age which felt the necessity of restoring the lost glory of the English stage and produced a great number of plays, did not formulate any such theory in a systematic manner; it is the task of posterity to piece the bits into a complete structure.

In 1843, while writing a short note on *The Borderers*, Wordsworth, in order to clarify his standpoint on the characterization of Oswald, tells us: "While I was composing this play, I wrote a short essay, illustrative of that constitution and those tendencies of human nature, which make the apparently motiveless actions of bad men intelligible to careful observers."[31] This "short essay" written either in late 1796 or early 1797 has been considered to be the Preface to the play in E.D. Selincourt's edition of Wordsworth's poetical works[32] and also in Prose Works of William Wordsworth edited by W.J.B. Owen and J.W. Smyser.[33] In that Preface, the author has offered a long philosophical discussion on the intricacies of human character by which "a young man of great intellectual powers" gets so much transformed that "to hunt out whatever is bad in actions usually esteemed virtuous, and to detect the good in actions which the universal sense of mankind teaches us to reprobate" becomes "his pleasure and his consolation."[34] Thus, Wordsworth starts with an unconventional and complicated issue and tries to convince others of his argument. It is evident that this Preface is widely different from his Preface to the *Lyrical Ballads* and also from the prefaces written by other romantic playwrights; and that is why Owen has called this Preface "unique among Wordsworth's critical writings" as "it is not concerned with poetics, with an account of the nature or the making of poetry." This Preface to *The Borderers*, Owen goes on to say, "is concerned with the analysis of a dramatic character whom the author feels to be potentially puzzling to the audience, and with an attempt to show that the characters psychologically credible in spite of contrary appearances." (*LC*, 8) So, here Wordsworth's primary contention is not about any dramatic theory, but his own theory of a particular character. Although this metaphysical obscurity is something puzzling to the readers and certainly to the audience, yet Wordsworth affirms it to be his first-hand experience, and connects the character of Oswald with "what I had observed of transition in character, and the reflections I had been led to make during the time I was a witness of the changes through which the French Revolution passed."[35] Of course, there is some dispute among the critics regarding the origin of this character and the relevance of this connection; and some critics have detected the literary antecedents for Oswald in the works of Godwin and in Gothic novels such as Mrs. Radcliffe's.[36]

However, the critical approach used here by Wordsworth is like that of character-analysis of Shakespearean characters, which was comparatively a recent vogue in Wordsworth's time. Nicol Smith comments: "The third quarter of the eighteenth century, and not the first quarter of the nineteenth, is the true period of transition in Shakespearean criticism— . . . there is a far reaching change in the literary appreciation of Shakespeare, which announces the school of Coleridge and Hazlitt: his characters now become the main topic of criticism."[37] Some of the eighteenth century critics like Joseph Warton, William Richardson and Maurice Morgann share a common platform in their approach to Shakesepeare's unusual or problematic characters whose dramatic credibility is their aim to defend. Since the critical effort is to reconcile seeming inconsistencies or to make the apparent improbabilities acceptable, the critic needs to identify a unifying element in the character in which the inconsistencies can be seen to be reconciled. Thus Richardson draws upon the eighteenth century concept of a ruling passion; in the case of Macbeth, it is ambition, the degree of which, or the degree of ascendancy of which, over repressive faculties, determines the behaviour of the character.[38] We are not certain of the fact that Wordsworth might have read all these critics by 1797, but all were available to him; and there is a peculiar similarity between the approach of these critics and that of Wordsworth. He also identifies a single intellectual trait in the character of Oswald to which his apparently motiveless actions may conform: "His master passions are pride and the love of distinction. . . . If. . . . I am asked what are Rivers's[39] motives to the atrocity detailed in the Drama? I answer: they are founded chiefly in the very constitution of his character; in his pride which borders even upon madness . . . in his perverted reason justifying his perverted instincts." (*LC*, 59, 63) Thus, ambition in Macbeth, or pride in Oswald dictates the actions of the character and accounts for the violent and total change in Macbeth, or the 'transition in character' in Oswald.

So far Wordsworth tries to make the seeming improbabilities acceptable and towards the end of his Preface he proceeds from the specific character to a generalized notion; and goes even to that extent where he says that Oswald's behaviour is credible because we behave in the same or in a comparable fashion: "It must be observed, that to make the non-existence of a common motive itself a motive to action is a practice which we are never so prone to attribute exclusively to madmen as when we forget ourselves. . . . We all know that the dissatisfaction accompanying the first impulses towards a criminal action, where the mind is familiar with guilt, acts as a stimulus to proceed in that action . . . in a course of criminal conduct every fresh step that we make appears a justification of the one that preceded it. . . . Every time we plan a fresh accumulation of our guilt, we have restored to us something like that original state of mind . . . which first made the crime attractive." (*LC*, 62-63) In this way, the author, by insinuating that in any case the character's behaviour can be recognized in our own behaviour, and by pointing out the ruling passion of the character, attempts to persuade us that his behaviour is intelligible and dramatically probable. How far he has been successful in his attempt is, undoubtedly, a debatable issue. But this much can be said that his metaphysical outlook poses a great problem to the theatre-going public whose primary aim is to get entertainment.

However obscure Wordsworth may be in his Preface, at least at one point he strikes an important note of which a repetition may be found in Charles Lamb. Wordsworth hints at a basically wrong assumption of the audience when he says that "we are too apt to apply our own moral sentiments as a measure of the conduct of others. We insensibly suppose that a criminal action assumes the same form to the agent as to ourselves. We forget that his feelings and his reason are equally busy in contracting its dimensions and pleading for its necessity." (*LC*, 64) Thus, he asks the audience to suppress their own moral inhibitions for the time being in order to have a proper understanding of a character. Lamb in his essay on the artificial comedy has made this point, though the context there is different. While Wordsworth speaks of tragedy, Lamb comments on comedies. Whatever may be the context, this argument is definitely true as it points at the basic principle of enjoying a work of art. Aesthetic experience and our sense of morality need not go hand in hand; morality is something which comes in our afterthought; not at the moment of enjoyment of a work of art.

Coleridge tasted the success of staging *Remorse* and *The Triumph of Loyalty* and translated two dramas of Schiller. About the two plays depicting the life and death of Wallenstein, Coleridge remarked: "These dramas have two grievous faults; they are prolix in the particular parts and slow in the general movement. But they have passion, distinct and diversified character; and they abound in passages of great moral and poetic beauty."[40] *Wallenstein*, the most Shakespearean of all German drama, clearly reflects Schiller's study of *Henry IV*, *Richard II* and *Richard III*, and Coleridge, in his note on the fly leaf of the annotated (in Coleridge's own handwriting) copy, criticised these plays using the Shakespearean standard; and the points on which he criticised may fairly be taken as his view on what a play, particularly tragedy, ought to be. Coleridge is right to assert that "we learn them [dramatic characters] from the actions and from the descriptions given by other characters or from particular speeches," but in Schiller's play, though "the characters are truly diversified and distinctly conceived," yet "the assassins who talk ludicrously are not "fearful and almost pitiable beings" like Macbeth, but "loathsome and ludicrous miscreants." Coleridge is very serious over the ludicrous treatment of supernatural element in a tragedy. Schiller has used astrology, which Coleridge thinks, "an undramatic superstition because it inspires no terror, and its foundation of imagination is overbuilt and concealed by its scientific superstructure, with other cause from the imagery," in a prophetic sense and "yet treated ludicrously." Coleridge makes a valuable comment on the art of characterisation when he says that in a successful tragic character there should be a proper lending of strength and weakness "as in Macbeth," and not an imposition—Schiller has drawn weakness imposing on itself the love of power for the sense of strength, "which is a fine conception in itself, but not tragic." "These are the chief defects," but for its grand and salutary moral influence "we must allow its great praise." (598)

Thus, Coleridge is against slow movement of the action, ludicrous treatment of the supernatural in a prophetic sense and an imposition of strength on a generally weak character; while he is for properly conceived characters, their well-proportioned speeches, and the moral aspect of the play. Now let us judge his own play *Remorse* according to the principles set by him.

In his preface to *Osorio*, confessing his weaknesses, Coleridge requests the critics not to consider it as "a miscarriage," because, it "furnished me with a most important lesson namely, that to have conceived strongly, does not always imply the power of successful execution." Coleridge misses this "power of successful execution" even after a lapse of sixteen years, when in 1813 he recasts *Osorio* and writes *Remorse*. The loopholes are still there—Ordonio is not properly developed and a sense of strength has been imposed on his generally weak nature. Of its plus points we may say that in an otherwise action-packed play the speeches are suited to the characters, Ordonio never behaves ludicrously. Coleridge has used the dream element (IV.i) in a prophetic sense which is psychologically true and accurate;[41] and this play also abounds in moral influence. The last lines of the play (V.i.285-94) clearly reflect the author's religious beliefs and we never miss the poet of Christabel.

Shelley, with his intense idealistic zeal, goes one step further when he says in *A Defence of Poetry* that the highest kind of drama should be absurd and its characters should typify certain ideas. He is totally against the naturalistic play because he thinks that in drama we should try to concretise some ideas which cannot be comprehended in our everyday life. For this purpose, Shelley has advocated the use of masks in a drama, because the mask typifies the character, not individualises him and saves the drama from being a monologue "where all the attention may be directed to some great master of ideal mimicry." About the ideal form of a drama Shelley goes back to Athens, "for the Athenians employed language, action, music, painting, the dance and religious institutions to produce a common effect in the representation of the highest idealisms of passion and of power." To him music and dancing are very important in a play—the language should be musical or highly poetical in order to transcend the limits of everyday speech, and dancing denotes the co-ordinated movement of the characters according to the central structural ideas which constitute the essence of drama. Despite his admiration of *King Lear*—as it represents certain basic human characteristics and is both typical and universal—Shelley has criticised Shakespeare for neglecting "a relation between the drama and religion," and particularly in this respect he prefers Calderon.[42]

While thus talking of drama as a form of art, Shelley is also 'modern' in his acceptance of "the modern practice of blending comedy with tragedy" which "is undoubtedly an extension of the dramatic circle"; but the comic interest, as in *King Lear* should be blended with the total structure of ideas, it should be "universal ideal and sublime." Again, as a critic of the age, Shelley hints at its infertility in the field of drama and tries to establish a link between literature and society. As to the reason of this barrenness, Shelley views that "in periods of the decay of social life, the drama sympathizes with that decay"; and thus he attributes the absence of good drama to the degenerated society. At this point, Shelley changes the office and character of the poet and he says that "the connection of poetry and social good is more observable in the drama than in whatever other form." The dramatist not only reflects the society, nor he holds a mirror to nature, but helps to mould it. Moreover, Shelley thinks that great dramas are beautiful poems: "The drama, so long as it continues to express poetry, is a prismatic and many-sided mirror, which collects the brightest rays of human nature and divides and reproduces them from the simplicity of their elementary forms, and touches them with majesty and beauty, and multiplies all that it reflects, and endows it with the power of propagating its light wherever it may fall." (237)

With this prologue, Shelley presents before us *Prometheus Unbound* and *Hellas*—two lyrical dramas—which are not dramas in the popular sense but in the sense of representing some ideas and a peculiar type of action which cannot be brought within the limitations of the stage. In spite of Shelley's claim to consider *Prometheus* as a drama,[43] it is universally regarded as a poem due to its lyrical fervour. Of course, Shelley is hesitant in calling *Hellas* a drama and he argues: "If I have called this poem a drama from the circumstance of its being composed in dialogue, the license is not greater than that which has been assumed by other poets who have called their productions epics, only because they have been divided into twelve or twenty-four books." So, excluding the form of the composition, Shelley himself regards it as a poem; and the reason behind treating this subject—both in *Prometheus* and in *Hellas* is that it "is insusceptible of being treated otherwise."[44] Shelley chooses the dramatic form only to express his ideology, and despite his abhorrence of didactic poetry, there is his indication at the "golden age" (*Hellas*) and the rejoicing of the emancipated universe (*Prometheus Unbound*) which breathes the typical Shelleyan doctrine that "mankind had only to will that there should be no evil, and there would be none."[45]

Although Shelley is against naturalistic plays in his theory, yet the story of *The Cenci* suggests to him "the conception of its fitness for a dramatic purpose" and he writes a tragedy—*The Cenci*—where he has "avoided with great care the introduction of what is commonly called mere poetry." In his preface, explaining his scheme, Shelley desists from converting it into the "cold impersonations" of his own mind in order to represent the characters "as they probably were"; and it is this naturalistic play which gives Shelley a success as a playwright. As a dry exhibition of this eminently fearful and monstrous story on the stage will be insupportable, Shelley "increases the ideal and diminishes the actual horror of the event, so that the pleasure which arises from the poetry which exists in these tempestuous sufferings and crimes may mitigate the pain of the contemplation of the moral deformity from which they spring." To present Beatrice as a real tragic character, Shelley does not bestow her with "revenge, retaliation and atonement" but develops her "proceeding from vehement struggle, to horror, to deadly resolution, and lastly to the elevated dignity of calm suffering, joined to passionate tenderness and pathos." Shelley is right to assert that it is "in the restless and anatomizing casuistry with which men seek the justification of Beatrice, yet feel that she has done what needs justification; it is in the superstitious horror with which they contemplate alike her wrongs and their revenge, that the dramatic character of what she did and suffered, consists"; and accordingly, he has drawn the character.

Again in this serious play which has no comic interlude, Shelley has tried to connect religion with drama. But religion here, as in the mind of an Italian Catholic, "is interwoven with the whole fabric of life. It is adoration, faith, submission, penitence, blind admiration; not a rule for moral conduct."[46] Lucretia's design in exposing herself to the consequences of an expostulation with Cenci after having administered the opiate (IV.i) is to induce him by a feigned tale to confess himself before death, and this confession is esteemed by Catholics as essential to salvation. Lucretia consoles her daughter:

> Trust in God's sweet love,
> The tender promises of Christ: ere night,
> Think, we shall be in Paradise. (V.iv.75-77)

Thus, religion casts an all-round spell over this tragedy and it gives a touch of solemnity which Shelley considers to be one of the essential ingredients of a great drama.

Keats who had got into only the second chamber of human life, the Chamber of Maiden Thought, and also groped for a permanent philosophy of life, had not enough scope or time to formulate a definite dramatic theory of his own. In comparison to Shelley, Byron and Coleridge, Keats is remarkably silent on this topic. Peculiarly enough, his only tragedy *Otho the Great* on which he depended much, is published without any preface where we might have a clue to his views. Perhaps when his play was refused to be staged both at Drury Lane and Covent Garden, Keats was greatly disappointed and he published it merely as a literary exercise and not as a full-fledged drama and that is why we have this indifference. However, if we go through his letters we may find some casual references to his views which are applicable better to a general idea on literature as a whole. His famous theory of Negative Capability[47] works well as a general theory of literature.

If we apply these views to drama in particular, we are surprised to note Keats' unconventional stand in an age where subjective treatment of the facts forms the main basis. To write a perfect drama, the author should maintain the precarious balance between self-involvement and a sense of detachment. His mind should be all inclusive where Sir Toby's epicurean philosophy easily co-exists with Jaques's cynicism and Malvolio's stern morality. The necessity of possessing such a mind to write a good drama has been stressed by none other than Keats; and only for this reason he can claim our attention.

Keats's letter to Shelley (dt. Aug. 1820) reviewing *The Cenci* hints at a certain 'discipline' which a dramatist should follow: "I received a copy of the 'Cenci'. . . . There is only one part of it I am judge of—the poetry and dramatic effect, which by many spirits now-a-days is considered the Mammon. A modern work it is said must have a purpose, which may be the God. An artist must serve Mammon; he must have 'self- concentration'—selfishness perhaps. You, I am sure, will forgive me for sincerely remarking that you might curb your magnanimity, and be more of an artist, and load every rift of your subject with ore." (266) Here most apologetically, Keats refers to Shelley's lofty idealism which prevents him from writing a good drama. Again, there is a reference to that painful reality of getting public appreciation and fame of which all the romantic writers were more or less scared.

Of all these poets, Byron stands apart in his overt rejection of the stage-conditions, as also in his utmost attempt to shake off the Shakespearean influence from English tragedy. Byron started out with the conviction that English tragedy could regain life only if it broke away from its Shakespearean models. Referring to *Sardanapalus* and *The Two Foscari* he delcared: "You will find all this very unlike Shakespeare; and so much the better in one sense, for I look upon him to be the worst of models, though the most extraordinary of writers."[48] The romantic imitation of the Elizabethans and Jacobeans seemed to him absurd. He said that *Marino Faliero* should not be judged "by your mad old dramatists . . . those turbid mountebanks—always expecting B. Jonson, who was a Scholar and a classic."[49] Whatever the audacity in these announcements, it is clear that he was trying to draw English drama away from Shakespeare and towards the classicism of Jonson. He saw no other means of rousing it from the grave. Writing to Murray in January 1821, Byron expressed the hope that English tragedy might indeed be revived "not . . . by following the old dramatists, who are full of gross faults, pardoned only for the beauty of their language; but by writing naturally and regularly, and producing regular tragedies, like the Greeks, but not in imitation, merely the outline of their conduct, adapted to our own times and circumstances." (57) It is this adaptation of the classic form to modern taste which Byron sought to bring about in his two Venetian tragedies and *Sardanapalus*.

Byron is classical in his strict observation of the "Unities." As he wrote to Murray on 16 February 1821: "It appears to me that good English—and a severer approach to the rules—might combine something not dishonourable to our literature." True to his proud temper Byron then boldly spoke of *Marino Faliero*: "I have also attempted to make a play without love.—And there are neither rings—nor mistakes—nor starts—nor outrageous ranting villains—nor melodrama—in it.—All this will prevent its popularity, but does not persuade me that it is therefore faulty." (78) Again, in his Preface to *Sardanapalus* and *The Two Foscari,* he clearly states: "The author has in one instance attempted to preserve and in the other to approach the 'Unities'; conceiving that with any very distant departure from them, there may be poetry, but can be no drama. He is aware of the unpopularity of this notion in present English literature; but it is not a system of his own, being merely an opinion, which not very long ago, was the law of literature throughout the world, and is still so in the more civilised parts of it."[50] Thus *Sardanapalus* became a virtuoso exercise in the observation of rigid neoclassic unities. Battles are fought inside palace-halls, and dynastic upheavals transpire in a matter of hours. In this play Byron wrote a dramatic blank verse from which the presence of Shakespeare has been entirely exorcised. It carries forward from the best of Ben Jonson:

> Why do I love this man? My country's daughters
> Love none but heroes. . . .
> The hour is coming when he'll need all love,
> And find none. (I.ii)

The plain, rapid monosyllables lay bare the sinews of the dramatic action. About *Marino Faliero*, Byron said elsewhere: "It is too regular—the time, twenty-four hours—the change of place not frequent—nothing melodramatic—no surprises, no starts, nor trapdoors, nor opportunities for 'tossing their heads and kicking their heels'—and no love—the grand ingredient of a modern play." (VII, 22-23) *Marino Faliero* failed totally when it was performed without the author's consent and Byron could realize that his style of drama would not achieve success on the contemporary stage. On 14 September 1821, he wrote to Lady Byron: "I am trying an experiment—which is to introduce into our language—the regular tragedy—without regard to the stage—which will not admit of it—but merely to the mental theatre of the reader." (VIII, 210) Thus, Byron wrote dramas which are to be read or at most to be recited formally in a style alien to the tradition of the English theatre.

Byron's "mystery plays," first major Biblical dramas since Milton, turn their back on realism and they are vast, epic presentations of the mystery of evil. They are pageants of the religious imagination, and here Byron is most profoundly un-Shakespearean. For it is one of the root principles of Shakespearean art that the religious element should be diffuse, provisional and internal to the poetry, rather than manifest in the plot or the moral. In a sense all the tragedies of Shakespeare are religious, but from them all assuagements of rite of explicit doctrine are cruelly absent. Byron, on the contrary, rejoins the tradition of the medieval mystery cycle.

In design, *Cain* and *Heaven and Earth* are futuristic. Concerned only with a theatre of the mind, Byron devised fantastic effects. The encounter between Lucifer and Cain, which is the centre of the play, is set in Hades and the Abyss of Space. No ordinary stage machinery could create the necessary illusion of stellar and oceanic vastness:

Cain: 'Tis like another world; a liquid sun—
And those inordinate creatures sporting
O'er its shining surface?
Lucifer: Are its inhabitants
The past leviathans. (II.ii)

Heaven and Earth is even further removed from the practical conventions of the theatre. In conversation with Thomas Medwin, Byron indicated how this drama was to end (what we have is only the first part): "Adah is momentarily in danger of perishing before the eyes of the Arkites. Japhet is in despair. The last wave sweeps her from the rock, and her lifeless corpse floats past in all its beauty, whilst a sea-bird screams over it, and seems to be the spirit of her angel lord."[51] Even in the extant version of the play, as the Deluge rises to the summits of the Caucasus, Japhet and the Chorus of Mortals cry out:

Some clouds sweep on as vultures for their prey,
While others, fixed as rocks, await the word
At which their wrathful vials shall be poured.
No azure more shall robe the firmament,
Nor spangled stars be glorious: Death hath risen:
In the sun's place a pale and ghastly glare
Hath wound itself around the dying air. (I.iii)

One hears behind the words organ peals and the blast of trumpets. Obviously early nineteenth century English stage was quite unable to represent such ideas and these effects may be fully realized on our present stage where the resources of the film and the microphone are combined. Thus, Byron sought deliberately to surmount the limitations of the traditional stage in order to attain freer, larger forms of symbolic action; and though his plays are generally regarded as ambitious failures, yet his late plays may be given a trial performance, perhaps on a stage specially designed for them.

When wishing to illustrate his own conception of tragedy, Byron said, "Take up a translation of Alfieri." (VIII. 57) This Italian dramatist, who, according to George Steiner, is perhaps, "the only major dramatic talent produced in Italy between Goldoni and Pirandello," (213) belongs to that school of drama which sought to combine classic forms with romantic values. In Byron, as in Alfieri, the neo-classic conventions run directly against the gain of an intensely lyrical and romantic temper; and this gives to Byron's plays their special quality; they have a kind of febrile coldness. In *Marino Faliero*, the contrast lies in its sumptuous romantic setting and the tough sparseness of the language. Doge Faliero meets Bertuccio, the chief of the conspirators, on the little square of San Giovannie San Paolo. Above them towers the monument to Colleoni:

Doge: We are observed, and have been
Bertuccio: We observed:
Let me discover—and this steel—
Doge: Put up;
Here are no human witnesses: look there—
What see you ?
Bertuccio: Only a tall warrior's statue
Bestriding a proud steed, in the dim light
Of the dull moon.
Doge: That warrior was the sire
Of my sire's fathers, and that statue was
Decreed to him by the twice rescued city:
Think you that he looks down on us or no?
Bertuccio: My lord, these are mere fantasies; there are
No eyes in marble.
Doge: But there are in Death (III.i)

Steiner is eloquent on this speech and remarks: "No one writing drama in English in the early nineteenth century could have equalled this piece of dialogue or found that Roman epithet "twice rescued," and "around the harsh classic action plays romantic moonlight." (205)

About the conception of a tragic hero, Byron wrote to Francis Hodgson: "I must remark from Aristotle and Rymer, that the hero of tragedy and a tragic poem must be guilty, to excite 'terror and pity,' the end of tragic poetry. But hear not me, but my betters." Then he quoted a few lines from Dryden's life in Johnson's *Lives of the Poets*: "The pity which the poet is to labour for is for the criminal—not for those or him he has murdered—as who have been the occasion of the Tragedy. The terror is likewise in the punishment of the said criminal, who, if he be represented too great an offender, will not be pitied; if altogether innocent his punishment will be unjust." (VIII, 115) Byron is undoubtedly loyal to this viewpoint as no one of his tragic heroes are either 'great offender' or 'altogether innocent'; he holds the balance, but still misses the true tragic grandeur.

However, it is undeniable that Byron in the early nineteenth century was the only figure who attempted to strike an original note in his way of thinking on drama. But the pride, the audacity which we have noticed in his letters of 1821 became remarkably subdued in 1822 and in his letter to B.W. Procter we hear a tone almost free from any sting: "My own notions on the subject of the English drama altogether are so very different from the popular ideas of the day, that we differ essentially (as indeed I do from our whole English literati) upon that topic; but I do not contend that I am in the right. I merely say that such is my opinion—and as it is a solitary one, it can do no great harm." (IX, 84) Though it contains a firm assertion of his individuality, one cannot miss the fact that the author is gradually receding backwards. Finally, he himself dampens the issue when on 5 March 1823, he writes to Procter: "As for myself neither my way of thinking on the subject as an art—nor probably my powers—are at all adapted for the English drama—nor did I ever think that they were." (X, 116) Whether this confession is due to his intellectual humbleness or his gentle weariness we do not know.

The most interesting point to note in the course of this study of Romantic drama is, generally, a sense of uncertainty over the success of the dramatic works of almost all the great romantic poets. In order to perform their self-imposed task to revitalize English drama, they tried their best but could not reach their cherished goal which resulted in a total avoidance of the stage; and this failure led them to renounce their own voice and living speech and to look back to Elizabethan England. Here again, we notice two opposite tendencies—on the one hand there is the slavish imitation of the past, and on the other there is the eagerness to shake off the Shakespearean precedent. Apart from the major romantic poets, we have Thomas Lovell Beddoes, a minor figure who despite writing plays completely penetrated into the language and technique of the Jacobeans, expressed most eloquently the need for independence: "With the greatest reverence for all the antiquities of the drama, I still think that we had better beget than revive—attempt to give the literature of this age an idiosyncrasy and spirit of its own, and only raise a ghost to gaze on, not to live with—just now the drama is a haunted ruin." Yet between this clear knowledge and the act of writing fell the Shakespearean shadow; and this fact takes us back to our proposition with which we started this chapter.

NOTES

1. *English Critical Texts 16th Century to 20th Century,* ed. E.J. Enright and E.D. Chickera (London: OUP, 1962), p. 238.
2. George Steiner, *The Death of Tragedy* (London, 1961), p. 108.
3. Letter to Byron, dt. 15 October 1815, *Collected Letters of S.T. Coleridge*, ed. E. L. Griggs, 6 Vols (London: OUP, 1956-71), Vol. IV, 1959, p. 598.
4. "Essay on Drama," *Prose Works of Sir Walter Scott*, 28 Vols. (Edinburgh, 1834-36), Vol. VI, p. 380.
5. *A History of English Drama* (1600-1900), 6 Vols., 1952-59 (Cambridge Univ. Press, 1955), Vol. IV, p. 59.
6. Nicoll says, "A sense of humour springs from the power of seeing two sides to a question, or, in other words from the power of seeing beyond oneself." *Ibid*, p. 61.
7. Translation by George Steiner, *The Death of Tragedy*, p. 136.
8. *Complete Works of John Keats*, ed. N.H. Dole (London, 1906), Vol. IV, pp. 39, 120-21, 134.
9. Preface to *The Cenci*. *Poetical Works of P.B. Shelley*, ed. T. Hutchin-

son, a new ed. corrected by G.M. Mathews (London, 1971, rpt. 1975), p. 276.

10. *John Woodvil*, Act V, *Complete Works of Charles Lamb* (Modern Library edition, New York, 1935), p. 457.
11. *The Borderers*, Act V, *The Complete Poetical Works of Wordsworth*, ed. A.J. George (Cambridge, 1932), p. 69.
12. *Remorse*, Act V, Sc. 1, *Complete Poetical Works of. S.T. Coleridge*, Vol. II, ed. E.H. Coleridge (Oxford, 1912), p. 876.
13. *Manfred*, Act III, Sc. IV, *The Poetical Works of Lord Byron*, ed. F. Page, a new ed., John Jump (London: OUP, 1970), p. 406.
14. *The Reflector*, No. iii, 1811.
15. Preface to *Marino Faliero, Poetical Works*, p. 408.
16. A. Nicoll, *A History of English Drama* (1600-1900), Vol IV, pp. 88-89.
17. *Ibid*., pp. 92-94 (footnotes).
18. Letter to Thomas Manning, dt. December 5, 1806, *Works*, p. 760.
19. Letter to Taylor, dt. 23 Aug 1819, *Poetical Works*, Vol. IV, p. 179.
20. *The Prose Works of William Wordsworth*, ed. Alexander B. Grosart, 3 Vols. (London, 1876), Vol. III, p. 13.
21. Letter dt. 15 Aug 1819. *Poetical Works*, Vol. IV, p. 176.
22. *Poetical Works of Shelley*, p. 337.
23. *Eliana; being the hitherto uncollected writings*,. ed. J.E. Babson, (London, 1864), p. 54.
24. P.C. Ghosh, *Poetry and Religion as Drama* (Calcutta, 1974), p. 11.
25. *Byron's Letters and Journals*, ed. L.A. Marchand, 12 Vols. (London, 1978), Vol. 8, p. 134.
26. *Poetical Works of Shelley*, p. 482.
27. *Ibid*., p. 410.
28. *Poetical Works*, pp. 598-99.
29. *Prose Works*, pp. 13-14.
30. This may appear to be a sweeping comment about dramas written by the great romantic poets. But the scheme and the scope of the present book do not allow me to go into the detailed discussion in order to substantiate the point. A curious reader may go through Allardyce Nicoll's. *A History of English Drama* (1660-1900), and also *The Theatre and Dramatic Theory* by the same author. George Steiner's *The Death of Tragedy* is another important work in this field.
31. *The Prose Works of William Wordsworth*, ed. Grosart, Vol. 3, p. 13.
32. *Poetical Works of William Wordsworth*, ed. E.D. Selincourt and H. Darbishire, 5 Vols. (Oxford, 1940-49), Vol. 1, pp. 345-49.

33. 3 Vols. (Oxford, 1974). Vol. 1, pp. 76-80.
34. *Wordsworth's Literary Criticism*, ed. W.J.B. Owen, (The Routledge Critics Series, London and Boston, 1974), p. 59. Abbreviated *LC* and incorporated into the text.
35. *Prose Works*, ed. A.B. Grosart, p. 13.
36. Introduction to the Preface of *The Borderers, Prose Works of William Wordsworth*, ed. W.J.B. Owen and J.W. Smyser, Vol. 1, pp. 69-74.
37. *Eighteenth Century Essays on Shakespeare*, ed. D. Nichol Smith (2nd ed., Oxford, 1963), pp. xxxii.
38. *Essays on Shakespeare's Dramatic Characters of Macbeth, Hamlet, Jacques and Imogen* (4th ed., London, 1785), pp. 45-46.
39. Rivers is the name given to Oswald in the play as represented by Selincourt's manuscript of the play and the Preface, Selincourt's edition of Wordsworth's *Poetical Works*, Vol. 1, pp. 343-44.
40. *Poetical Works*, p. 598.
41. Coleridge has justified his treatment of dream-element in this way: "Prophetical dreams are things of nature and explicable by that law of the mind where dim ideas are connected with vivid feelings. Perception and Imagination insinuate themselves and mix with the forms of Recollection, till the present appears to exactly correspond with the Past. Whatever is partially like, the Imagination will gradually represent as wholly like—a law of our nature which when it is perfectly understood, woe to the great city Babylon—to all the superstitions of Men." *Poetical Works*, p. 566, fn.
42. Shelley's "Defence of Poetry," *English Critical Texts*, ed. Enright and Chickera, pp. 235-38.
43. "My *Prometheus Unbound* is just finished. . . . It is a drama with characters and mechanism of a kind yet unattempted," Shelley wrote from Rome after completing his drama. Notes by Mrs. Shelley, *Poetical Works*, p. 274.
44. Preface to *Hellas*, *Poetical Works*, p. 446.
45. Notes on *Prometheus Unbound* by Mrs. Shelley, *Ibid.*, p. 271.
46. *Poetical Works*, pp. 276-77.
47. *The Complete Works of John Keats*, ed. N.H. Dole, 4 Vols. (Laurel Edition, London and Boston, 1906), Vol. IV, p. 39.
48. Letter to John Murray, dt. 14 July 1821, *Byron's Letters and Journals*, ed. L.A. Marchand, Vol. 8, p. 152.
49. Letter to John Murray, dt. 4 January 1821, *Ibid.*, p. 57.
50. *Poetical Works*, p. 543.
51. Qtd. George Steiner, *The Death of Tragedy*, p. 210.

The Poet as Dramatist: A Study of Keats's *Otho the Great*

JIBESH BHATTACHARYYA

John Keats, a self-taught genius, is well-known as a great Romantic poet of England. In his very brief literary career (1816-1820) his output is astounding. Moreover, he attained maturity in this sphere with an incredible rapidity. Jack Stillinger observes: "He [Keats] had the shortest writing career of any of the major poets in English, and without question the fastest development."[1] It is a pity that Keats died young. Had he lived longer, his genius would have displayed its eminence not only in the sphere of poetry, but in other branches of literature as well. Graham Hough's observation in this connection is worth noting: "Keats's work is always changing and developing. At his death he seems to have been on the edge of a further stage of growth. If Shelley had lived longer there would have been more Shelley, but probably more of the same kind. We feel of Keats that there was much to come that would have been new and different."[2] In fact, his ability as a dramatist was going to show itself when he had to leave this world with its "weariness, the fever, and the fret" for the grove of "embalmed darkness" where his immortal nightingale sings for ever.

Indeed, we wonder at the poet's power of creating a five-act tragedy in the manner of a great Elizabethan dramatist. In the Elizabethan age the stage provided many a writer with a living. So, a large number of plays were written in that period. But, in the early nineteenth century when there were several restrictions on the presentation of a drama, when the two playhouses 'Covent Garden' and 'Drury Lane' had the monopoly for the performance of serious drama, and when the people were not much inclined to go to theatre, it was almost impossible to expect that dramatic literature should thrive. Yet in this age plays were written by most romantic poets. However, very few of them achieved success as stage plays. "Keats was right to be sure that dramatic poetry was the supreme species of the art; Wordsworth was right to judge that it was no longer possible to write,"[3] observes William Walsh. Wordsworth and Coleridge could not be successful in the theatre with their plays *Borderers* and *Remorse* respectively. Byron, despite his too much egoism, displayed his dramatic talent in his *Manfred* and *Cain*. Shelley in his *Cenci* and *Prometheus Unbound* showed his notable achievement in blending poetry and drama. But none of them was successful in attracting the popular taste which hungered for Gothic tales and horror themes. The age, thus, was not congenial to the revival of drama. William Walsh rightly observes: "the tradition of poetic drama had been dead too long to allow a revival, even by someone with Keats's gifts, his enthusiasm for the stage, his dramatic imagination, and his profound feeling for Shakespeare." (115)

Keats's attention was drawn to drama after he had composed *Endymion*, *Hyperion*, *Lamia*, *The Eve of St. Agnes* and the great *Odes*. Compared to the other plays of the period, Keats's first attempt at writing for the stage is the product of mature genius. Had he lived and continued writing for the stage, "he might well have matured his knowledge into a successful dramatic talent."[4] Keats himself wrote to B. Bailey: "It was the opinion of most of my friends that I should never be able to write a scene. I will endeavour to wipe away the prejudice."[5] His play, *Otho the Great*, did not, however, get the recognition it deserved at the hands of the critics. He had written a good number of poems so far, and had found a niche for himself in the field of romantic poetry. And therefore, when he strayed from his wonted course to the new avenue of plays, critics viewed it with eyes of doubt and mistrust. But Keats was optimistic of his success. He wrote to George and Georgiana Keats: "I have finished a tragedy [*Otho the Great*] which if it succeeds will enable me to sell what I may have in manuscript to a good a(d)vantage."[6] The play was accepted for presentation at 'Drury Lane' with a promise of coming out 'next season.' Keats was elated at the prospect. He wrote to Fanny Keats: "My hopes of success in the literary world are now better than ever."[7]

In his tragedy *Otho the Great*, Keats treats a Gothic story dealing with the revolt against the tenth-century Holy Roman emperor Otho I ("the Great"). Conrad, Duke of Franconia, is the villain of the piece. He, along with prince Ludolf, son of Otho, revolts against the emperor. Later he is reunited with Otho in friendship by defeating Otho's enemy Gersa, the prince of Hungary.

Otho the Great is pre-eminently a tragedy of intrigue. Its action and catastrophe depend largely on intrigues hatched by the ambitious brother and sister, Conrad and Auranthe. Conrad, ambitious to thrive with the help of the emperor, tactfully befriends him although he openly revolts against the emperor. The emperor is large-hearted enough to forget and forgive Conrad's past rebellion and as a sign of friendship offers to get his son Ludolf married to Conrad's sister, Auranthe. Auranthe, however, has an affair with Albert, a knight favoured by Otho. But, learning from her brother that the emperor wants her to be his daughter-in-law, she is willing to give up Albert for becoming the future queen of the country. In order to appear pure and chaste before everybody she has, by a contrivance, made Erminia, niece of Otho, appear to have been involved in the affair in which, in reality, she herself is involved. But, as ill luck would have it, her secret design against Erminia accidentally comes to be known by the latter from a letter in which Auranthe discloses the matter to her brother, Conrad. Erminia seeks the help of Albert to bring the matter to the notice of the emperor by carrying the letter secretly written by Auranthe to her brother.

Erminia herself comes to Otho in the company of Ethelbert, an abbot, who charges Auranthe, who is now already married to Ludolf, with contriving the plot to stain the honour and good name of the noble and pure Erminia. Ethelbert wants to present a sound proof of his accusation through Albert. Now Albert is called. But, instead of corroborating the statement of Ethelbert, he exclaims: "what proof should I have 'gainst a fame/ Impossible to slur?" (III.ii.216-17) And this is because he still loves Auranthe and so he does not want to harm her by disclosing her secret letter. Later, when he meets her, he says: "Your safety I have bought to-day/ By blazoning a lie." (IV.i.141-42) And he gives her a chance to escape a horrible end by eloping with him. But, if she does not agree, her fate will be in his hand. As he goes out, the brother and the sister plan to get rid of this canker. Conrad thinks that if Albert is kept alive, there is no safety for them, and so he must be killed. But, Auranthe is against the murder. Yet, both decide to meet Albert in the woods where Albert said he would be waiting for Auranthe. At night Auranthe escapes. Ludolf, who has been keeping a strict vigil over his newly wed wife, learns from his page that both Conrad and Auranthe have secretly left the castle. Gersa, the prince of Hungary, who is present there, informs that Albert, too, has left. Ludolph now burns with rage. He rushes out to meet Auranthe and takes revenge for the betrayal. He cries out: "Burn—burn the witch!" (IV.ii.139) In the forest he finds Albert wounded. Albert says that he has been wounded by Conrad. Soon Auranthe comes there and laments for Albert. Albert dies and Auranthe is taken home by Ludolph. Then in a short scene we are informed through conversation of some officers of the court that Conrad is dead and that prince Ludolph has gone mad and he "fills the arched rooms/ With ghastly ravings." (V.iii.15-16) The play ends with the deaths of Auranthe and Ludolph in a mysterious manner. Ludolph loved Auranthe's true nature that kills him. And Auranthe dies, probably being unable to bear the mental strain for the apprehended punishment that may be meted out to her for practising deception on Otho and Ludolph.

Thus, an analysis of the plot makes it clear that it is a network of intrigue. Conrad starts the intrigue against Otho the Great, who is noble enough to be easily duped. In a magnanimous manner he proposes his son's marriage with Conrad's sister, not knowing the true nature of that woman. Ludolph also becomes enamoured of Auranthe's beauty and accepts her as his wife. We also hear of Auranthe's intrigue against Erminia in order to shift her own guilt to the latter. Then there is the intrigue against Albert by Conrad, who, in order to be safe, wants Albert to be killed. And finally there is the intrigue of Albert to take Auranthe away from her husband by a threat to disclose her secret plot against Erminia to the emperor. All these intrigues have been very subtly managed by Keats like a finished dramatic artist.

The play is a typical example of Keats's Hellenism. Keats was a Greek without knowing Greek. In this play Keats observes many of the classical rules and conventions. The play maintains the three classical unities of time, place and action. The incidents of the play occur in and around the castle of Friedburg. The duration of these incidents, as stated by Keats himself, is but "one day." Thus, it does not exceed the classical limit of twenty-four hours. The unity of theme or action is maintained by the absence of any sub-plot. All the incidents ultimately lead to the intense suffering of the emperor Otho because of the tragic end of his dear son, Ludolf. Apart from the maintenance of the classical rules of the unities, *Otho the Great* maintains the Aristotelian principle that a play must have a beginning, a middle and an end with the scenes distributed proportionately among these parts. In *Otho the Great* these three parts are properly balanced. The first act may rightly serve as the exposition. Here we meet most of the important characters and learn of the Iagoesque Conrad's plan of dispatching Albert, Auranthe's erstwhile paramour, and thriving on the emperor's favour. Conrad tells his sister, Auranthe, a co-sharer of his ambitious design: "Have I not laboured, plotted?" (I.i.109) To this Auranthe replies:

> 'Twas for yourself you laboured—not for me!
> Do you not count, when I am queen, to take
> Advantage of your chance discoveries
> Of my poor secrets, and so hold a rod
> over my life? (I.i.112-16)

Conrad's villainous nature is revealed here. In the second act the complication takes shape as we find Erminia, Otho's niece, discovering the vile scheme of Auranthe to involve her falsely in an immoral affair. The situation reaches the climax in the second scene of the third act where Ethelbert, an abbot, comes with Erminia and seeks justice from Otho. Ethelbert accuses Auranthe and her brother of falsely implicating Erminia in a sex scandal in which, in reality, Auranthe herself is involved. He wants to tell "the names of those vipers, from whose jaws/ A deadly breath went forth to taint and blast/This guileless lady [Erminia]." (III.ii.153-55) But a cloud of suspense is raised as Albert, the possessor of a letter written by Auranthe containing the sure proof of her villainy declines to bring any charge against Auranthe. Now things begin to move very quickly. Albert appears before Auranthe and asks her to elope with him or else meet her ruin at his hands. Ludolph, who keeps keen watch on his newly wed wife Auranthe, finds her missing from the castle. All rush to the nearby forest where Albert being wounded dies and Conrad is reported dead. Ludolph brings Auranthe home and helpless Auranthe dies of shock and shame. Ludolph goes mad and dies. Thus, the play is brought to its inevitable end most naturally.

Apart from observing the classical rules of architectural design, Keats also follows another convention of the classical tragedy, which emphasizes the sway of fate. This is secured in the play by the accident of the letter of Auranthe being lost and recovered by Erminia, an incident that may remind one of the loss of the handkerchief by Desdemona and its recovery by Emilia in Shakespeare's *Othello*. Of course, the situations in the two plays are not quite similar. But in Keats's play, by the caprice of this incident the villainy of the brother and the sister is exposed. Erminia's entrusting Albert with that fateful letter also complicates the plot and hastens the end of the play. Besides conforming to the principles of a classical drama, the play fulfils the general requirement of dramatic structure consisting in a skilled intermixture of suspense and irony. Tragic irony is at work in Erminia's handing over Auranthe's secret letter to Albert with the expectation that he will vindicate her cause. Suspense and surprise are employed in the catastrophe. The sudden death of both Auranthe and Ludolph was not expected. The dark pall of tragedy comes over the stage with the quiet passing away of Ludolph at the end.

The classical tragedy avoids violence on the stage. All deaths and murders are generally reported. In this play also the deaths of Conrad and Auranthe are reported while deaths of Albert and Ludolph are free from any violence, at least on the stage. Keats has also employed the device of the chorus in the form of the three officers, Sigifred, Theodore and Gonfred who inform the audience, through their conversation, of many incidents and fasts which not only help the audience understand the play better, but also helps in the continuity and compactness of the plot structure.

The characters in the play, though not many, have been drawn with proper skill and insight, although some critics may think otherwise. Otho the Great has been presented as a really great, magnanimous, wide-hearted, just ruler and loving father. In his dealing with Conrad, Gersa and Ludolph these features come out very prominently. Conrad and Auranthe appear as ambitious contrivers and selfish hypocrites. We are made aware of these features of the brother and the sister from the very beginning of the play. Ludolph is a valiant fighter and an obedient son with filial piety. He revolts against his father, but realizing his folly he becomes repentant and is finally reconciled with his father. He seems to be a bit emotional and sentimental in his attitude to Auranthe. But that only shows the sincerity and genuineness of his love for Auranthe. Erminia in her brief appearance has maintained her dignity as the niece of the great emperor. She is greatly shocked when Albert, in whom she has put her trust, betrays her. Ethelbert, the abbot, has been portrayed as a true well-wisher of the royal family. With a powerful but restrained speech, just becoming a man of the religious order, he argues the case of Erminia before the emperor. Thus, in the creation of characters Keats has shown his ability to make the men and women living and convincing.

The romantic mind of Keats reveals itself in the beautiful poetic speeches he has given to some of his characters. In the opening scene Conrad muses: "Nor yet has/ My ship of fortune furl'd her silken sails." (I.i.4-5) Auranthe, on receiving the news from her brother that the emperor has chosen her as the wife of his son, Ludolph exclaims:

> Thou, Jove-like, struck'st thy forehead,
> And from the teeming marrow of thy brain
> I spring complete Minerva! (I.i.93-95)

Emperor Otho, after releasing Gersa, the prince of Hungary and prisoner of war, says: "And thus a marble column do I build/ To prop my empire's dome." (I.ii.160-61) Ludolph who has fallen in love with Auranthe longs to meet his lady-love and says: "those turreted Franoconian walls,/ Like to a jealous casket, hold my pearl/ My fair Auranthe!" (I.iii.102-4) Ethelbert waxes eloquent about Erminia when Gersa expresses his doubt about her purity. He says that she cannot be false:

> Whom I have known from her first infancy,
> Baptiz'd her in the bosom of the Church,
> Watch'd her, as anxious husbandmen the grain,
> From the first shoot till the unripe mid-May,
> Then to the tender ear of her June days,
> Which, lifting sweet abroad its timid green,
> Is blighted by the touch of calumny. (II.ii.132-38)

Gersa also is charmed by the beauty of Erminia and praises her:

> The swan, soft leaning on her fledgy breast,
> When to the stream she launches, looks not back
> With such a tender grace; nor are her wings
> So white as your soul is. (II.ii.102-5)

In the fourth act Auranthe soliloquizes as her villainy is exposed by Ethelbert:

> O, thou golden Crown,
> Orbing along the serene firmament
> Of a wide empire, like a glowing moon;
> And thou, bright sceptre! lustrous in my eyes,—
> There—as the fabled fair Hesperian tree,
> Bearing a fruit more precious! graceful thing,
> Delicate, godlike, magic! must I leave
> Thee to melt in the visionary air. (IV.i.78-85)

When Ludolph in his frenzy talks of delicious wine :

> let me see—what wine?
> The strong Iberian juice, or mellow Greek?
> Or pale Calabrian? Or the Tuscan grape? (V.v.119-21)

The lines echo the second stanza of "Ode to a Nightingale" where the poet speaks of delicious wine by drinking which he wants to leave this world unseen by others.

Though the play is scattered with beautiful poetic speeches, they are not as emotional and sensuous as the exquisite romantic effusions in Keats's marvellous poems. This restraint adds much to the realistic and dramatic effect of the speeches and makes the drama stage-worthy, unlike Shelley's "Prometheus Unbound" which is nothing but an excellent lyric.

Towards the end of his life Keats became very much interested in drama and read the plays of Shakespeare with interest. Caroline F.E. Spurgeon makes a thorough study of Keats's reading of Shakespeare in her book *Keats's Shakespeare: A Descriptive Study.* There she most cogently observes: "Keats and Shakespeare had a very unusual, a very close and subtle relationship. They were alike in certain qualities of mind and of art, a fact of which Keats himself was fully aware, and in some of these qualities they are unique among English poets."[8] R.S. White also acknowledges Keats's debt to Shakespeare as he writes: "Keats could hardly have written a complete, five-act tragedy without drawing somewhere upon his acknowledged mentor [Shakespeare] in the field."[9]

But Keats has not based his tragedy on Shakespeare alone. He, perhaps, has in mind the plays of Beaumont and Fletcher particularly *A King and No King* and *The Maid's Tragedy* as far as his method of constructing the plot around a series of intricate relationships instead of concentrating upon one tragic protagonist is concerned. In *Otho the Great* although Ludolph is the tragic protagonist, he is not given much importance and the play is named after the emperor, Otho, as we find in naming the Shakespearean play, *Julius Caesar*. This particular aspect has attracted the attention of H.R. Beaudry who remarks, "there is no particularly outstanding character in the play as a whole, . . . each major personage is able to hold the reader's interest"[10] at some stage of the action. Yet, the tragic end of Ludolph caused by the betrayal of Auranthe, just as the ruin of the 'Knight-at-arms' brought about by the 'fairy's child' in "La Belle Dame Sans Merci," touches the sympathetic chord in the hearts of the readers and spectators alike.

The play is both a tragedy of love for Ludolph and a tragedy of ambition for Conrad and Auranthe. In a sense, it may be said to be a combination of *Othello* and *Macbeth*. But the intense passion displayed by Shakespeare in these plays has been much mellowed down in this play. Although the play may not have attained the height of excellence of a great Shakespearean tragedy, yet considering that it is the maiden attempt of the poet to write for the stage, "*Otho the Great* may yet be judged as an effective drama written in the vein of plays which had been enormously popular in the early seventeenth century, and which Keats admired."[11]

NOTES

1. Jack Stillinger, ed., *The Poems of John Keats* (London: Heinemann, 1978), p. 1.
2. *The Romantic Poets* (1953; rpt. London: Arrow, 1961), p. 157.
3. William Walsh, *Introduction to Keats* (London: Methuen, 1981), p. 115.
4. B. Ifor Evans, *A Short History of English Drama* (London: Penguin, 1948), p. 144.
5. Maurice Buxton Forman, ed., *The Letters of John Keats* (Humphrey Milford, OUP, 1931), vol. II, p. 399.
6. *Ibid.*, p. 434.
7. *Ibid.*, p. 485.
8. (1928; rpt. Oxford: Clarendon Press, 1966), pp. 53-54.
9. R.S.White, *Keats as a Reader of Shakespeare* (London: The Athlone Press, 1987), p. 205.
10. *The English Theatre of John Keats* (Salzburg, 1973), p. 184.
11. R.S. White, p. 206.

Contributors

N.M. Aston, Nowrosjee Wadia College, Pune

Jibesh Bhattacharya, Calcutta

M.N. Chatterjee, Umeschandra College, Calcutta

C.R. Das, University of Pune

A.M. Deshpande, University of Pune

L.S. Deshpande, Nanded

K.S. Iyer, T.C. College, Baramati

S. Kannamal, Vellalar College for Women, Erode

A.T. Kenghe, K.T.H.M. College, Nashik

R.S. Kimbahune, Marathwada University, Aurangabad

Zeenat B. Merchant, Poona College, Pune

M.K. Naik, Formerly Karnatak University, Dharwad

A. Nerlekar, Symbiosis College, Pune

Vivek D. Phadke, Fergusson College, Pune

Robert Pinto, Allahabad

Prabha Sampath, St. Mira's College, Pune